Source Music
in Motion Pictures

Source Music
in Motion
Pictures

Irene Kahn Atkins

Rutherford • Madison • Teaneck
Fairleigh Dickinson University Press
London and Toronto: Associated University Presses

Associated University Presses, Inc.
4 Cornwall Drive
East Brunswick, N.J. 08816

Associated University Presses Ltd
27 Chancery Lane
London WC2A 1NF, England

Associated University Presses
Toronto M5E 1A7, Canada

Library of Congress Cataloging in Publication Data

Atkins, Irene Kahn, 1922–
    Source music in motion pictures.

    Bibliography: p.
    Includes index.
    1. Moving-picture music—History and criticism.
I. Title.
ML2075.A85   1982   782.8'5   81-65338
ISBN 0-8386-3076-6

Printed in the United States of America

In the section "Songs in Films of the American Past" use is made of the author's article "The Melody Lingers On," which was published, in a slightly different form, in *Focus on Film*, no. 26, © The Tantivy Press, London, England, 1977. Used here by permission of the copyright holder.

To my mother,
ninety years young,
and always ready to see a new movie
and enjoy its music

Contents

List of Tables

Acknowledgments

I wish to thank the many people who provided information and suggestions, who gave me access to musical and cinematic material, and who opened their homes and offices in the interests of research:

Harry Lojewski and Ruby Armstrong of Metro-Goldwyn-Mayer Studios; Lionel Newman and Elena Vassar of Twentieth Century–Fox Studios; Frank Banyai of United Artists Music Company; David Jacobs of Chappell Music, Inc.; Mildred Simpson, Bonnie Rothbart, Terry Roach, and the staff of the Margaret Herrick Library of the Academy of Motion Picture Arts and Sciences; Anne Schlosser and the staff of the Charles K. Feldman Library of the American Film Institute; Audrée Malkin and the staff of the UCLA Theater Arts Library; David Bradley, Jack Clayton, Mrs. Henry Ephron, the late Bryan Foy, the late Hugo Friedhofer, Mr. and Mrs. Ira Gershwin and their special assistant, Michael Feinstein, John Green, Regina Gruss, Arthur Hamilton, Dr. Mantle Hood, Bronislaw Kaper, Helen and Ernst Korngold, Marvin Maazel, Ellen Malta, Stephen Mamber, Mrs. Charles Maxwell, Marjorie Ann Newby, David Raksin, Rico Ricardi, Nelson Riddle, and Robert Rosen.

Thanks also to Andrew Marx for his helpful collaboration, in 1971, on the research paper that first sparked my interest in source music, "They Shot the Last Horse at the Picture Show, Didn't They?" and to Leonard Atkins for sharing his tremendous musical knowledge with me.

Lastly, although I cannot thank him personally, I would

like to acknowledge the help of the late James Powers, director of publications for the American Film Institute and West Coast editor of *American Film* magazine, whose encouragement and constructive criticism actually made this book evolve.

Introduction

Source music is a type of motion picture music that has been heard in countless films, and that has enhanced the dramatic and emotional content of many of them. In the wealth of literature about film music, however, there has been little discussion of this type of music, and most glossaries of film terminology have been notably lacking in a definition of the term. Robert Emmett Dolan defines source music as "music, the origin of which is visually justified on the screen, as for example, to see and hear someone playing the piano in a film."[1]

This definition does not take into account music from sources that are unseen on the screen. A more precise definition of source music would be music that, whether emanating from a source visible on the screen (such as a musical instrument or ensemble, a vocalist, a radio, a record player, or a television receiver) or not, is assumed to be audible to the characters in the film.

Such film music, of course, would not include "underscoring" music. As Dolan states, the source music is justified, perhaps for the benefit of those skeptics who might ask, as Alfred Hitchcock is said to have done concerning *Lifeboat* (1944), where the music is coming from. (Composer David Raksin's reply was "Ask Mr. Hitchcock to explain where the cameras come from, and I'll tell him where the music comes from.")[2]

Both Dolan's definition and Hitchcock's question, apocryphal or not, raise the issue of whether film music needs to be justified at all, and the more complicated question of just what the function of film music is. Most discussions of the function or functions of film music are discussions about background scoring, and a satisfactory explanation has not really been offered in the literature. It is not the purpose of this work to discuss background scoring. The fact that source music usually is justified makes its functions—the imparting of information to and the evocation of emotional response from the audience—more readily discernible than those of other film music.

Dr. Robert U. Nelson, emeritus professor of music at UCLA, wrote for *Hollywood Quarterly* an article in which he presented a short but valuable discussion of source music, in the course of an analysis of film music that evokes a certain response from the audience because of its color.[3] The quavering notes of the zither turning out "The Third Man Theme" and the hurdy-gurdy in the New Orleans street in *Saratoga Trunk* (1946) were examples cited by Dr. Nelson as source music providing color. Dissonant harmonies or electronic instruments often provide color, too, but usually in the form of background scoring, not as source music.

The categories of background scoring and source music are logical ones into which all film music can be divided. A subtype of background scoring that is closely allied to source music is source scoring. Source scoring is music, often a song, that is heard first as source music and subsequently as background music, usually reorchestrated and in greatly expanded form. A famous example occurs in *Casablanca* (1943). The song "As Time Goes By" is first sung and played, simply and straightforwardly, by Dooley Wilson in a nightclub scene. During the remainder of the film, composer Max Steiner and orchestrator Hugo Friedhofer use the melody, or fragments of it, in lushly orchestrated music cues behind many of the most dramatic and romantic scenes in the film.[4]

With film music divided into these two broad categories, source music and background music, it is necessary, in order to define the limits of this book, to give some special consideration to the categorization of the musical film. In the broadest terms, there are only two types of film musicals: the "backstage musical" and the "book show." In the traditional backstage musical, all musical numbers fit into the definition of source music. There is a justification for the song or dance number. The other type of traditional musical, the book show, is a kind of cinematic operetta— *The Sound of Music* (1965) and other Rodgers and Hammerstein productions are typical—in which the music is an integral part of the drama, and singers burst into song spontaneously, with the orchestral accompaniment coming from nowhere, without the slightest attempt to justify the source of that accompaniment. The book show, so popular in the days of movie operettas, especially those featuring Jeanette MacDonald and Nelson Eddy, has not fared so well in the 1970s. Even by the end of the 1960s, the success of a film such as *Oliver* (1968) was offset by the failures of *On a Clear Day You Can See Forever*, (1970), *Thoroughly Modern Millie* (1967), and *Finian's Rainbow* (1968), all examples of the operetta format.

The fact that the book show has only fairly recently waned in popularity can be further substantiated by noting the fact that of the nine film musicals that have won the Academy Award for Best Picture since the award was established in 1927, all but two would be classed as book shows. *Broadway Melody* (1928–29) and *The Great Ziegfeld* (1937) were backstage stories. The other winners were *Going My Way* (1945), *An American in Paris* (1951), *Gigi* (1958), *West Side Story* (1961), *My Fair Lady* (1964), *The Sound of Music* (1965), and *Oliver* (1968).

In the backstage musical, the film audience sees some sort of show within a show. This is the form that most musicals of the 1970s have taken. *Cabaret* (1972), *A Star Is Born* (1976), and *New York, New York* are recent examples. So, in a broad sense, are *Bound for Glory* (1976) and *Nashville* (1975), although they might better be described as borderline cases, the so-called dramas with music.

One difficulty encountered in a consideration of the musical drama is the fact that the musical environments tend to diffuse the evaluation of the source music's function, being somewhat overpowering in their pervasiveness. In the dramatic nonmusical motion picture, source music functions in various ways to enhance the narrative action of the film. In such films, even when the music is most effective, it must of necessity remain adjunctive to the delineation of the plot and development of character. Yet, at the same time, the source-music usage becomes more challenging and offers a more propitious task for the composer or musical director.

In a discussion of source music, particularly in today's climate of "sound-track hits," another factor should be considered: the filmmaker's motivation for presenting musical numbers as part of the film. If the producer is concerned with exploiting a dramatic picture through records, air play, or the possibility of an Academy Award for an inserted song, there will probably be a musical number, particularly if the lead in the film is also well known as a singer. Certainly the scene can be presented so that it enhances the narrative emotionally as well as musically, but too often the performance of the song will cause a break in plot continuity. Such an interruption may add to the film's profits by virtue of record revenues, but aesthetically it can be damaging to the motion picture itself.

In at least two films, one of them famous as "the first talkie," the presence of a singing leading man changed the character of the film itself.[5] *The Jazz Singer* (1927) originally was to have starred George Jessel, who was a Broadway star but was not especially noted as a vocalist. Al Jolson's fame rested more on his singing than on his dramatic ability. When he took over the lead in *The Jazz Singer,* the highlight as well as the climax of the film was his performance of "Kol Nidre." He also sang several popular songs. (A year later Warner Brothers would purchase three major music-publishing companies so that they could use their own songs in pictures.) Leo McCarey had originally planned to direct Spencer Tracy in *Going My Way* (1944). The film, starring Bing Crosby, has been classed as a musical, but the numbers were all introduced in a natural way that helped insure the film's success but did not impede the story line. The film's Academy Award–winning "Swinging on a Star" (words: Johnny Burke; music: Jimmy Van Heusen) was the hit song of 1944–45.

Such examples, however, are counterbalanced by the dragged-in-by-the-heels presence of "We May Never Love like This Again" (music and lyrics by Al Kasha and Joel Hirschhorn) in *The Towering Inferno* (1974) or "The Morning After" (music and lyrics by Al Kasha and Joel Hirschhorn) in *Poseidon Adventure* (1972). (Both won Academy Awards.) And the "gold-record syndrome" seems to be becoming more prevalent rather than less so.

In any evaluation of the use of source music in films, it becomes evident that throughout the sound era there have been countless examples of its usage. Merely to enumerate these examples would be a mechanical exercise in cataloging. Rather, this work is organized into three major sections, designed in turn—

1. To show the way in which source music can enhance the dramatic elements in a film, and just how the music functions within the film itself. This sort of function is dealt with in detail in the section on old songs in nostalgia films, of which there have been numerous examples in recent years.

2. To discuss both the functions within the films and the intrinsic musical merits of certain compositions written for source-music sequences in specific motion pictures. The, emphasis here is on the possibility of finding—or rediscovering—musical material that could make a worthwhile addition to concert or recital repertoire.

3. To discuss some of the problems faced by the composer or musical director and the producer or director in selecting or composing material for source-music sequences in which the music is "ethnic" or "historical"—i.e., non-Western in character. The films chosen for this part of the study also manifested problems and methods of solving them that were typical of the ways in which the

studio system operated in its heyday, and thus information is provided that is related to dealings of the film composer with the major studios at that time.

As an introduction to the study of these problems, two sections deal with (1) the musical and nonmusical elements that make up a source-music scene and sequence, and (2) a historical overview of the use of source music throughout the sound era (1926 to the present). The historical section focuses on periods in film history when source-music usage was either very pronounced or sharply curtailed, and studies the reasons for such increases and decreases in usage.

The objective throughout is to present aspects of ways in which source-music has contributed—and can contribute—to the artistic and entertainment value of a motion picture.

Source Music
in Motion Pictures

1
Elements of the Source-Music Sequence

In the analysis of a source-music sequence, categorization of the musical and nonmusical elements serves as an aid in determining just how the scene and its music communicate with the audience.

The nonmusical elements are the visual, the dramatic, and the narrative (two or three of which may be present simultaneously). These elements are largely determined in answer to one of two questions: "Why is the source music necessary to the scene?" or, if the music is not really necessary, "Does its inclusion still add something dramatically and emotionally?"

Generally, the raison d'être of the source music will fall into one of three categories:

1. One or more of the chief protagonists is a musician—a composer, performer, or combination of the two. In this case there will probably be several scenes in which source music is heard and the performers seen.

2. One of the protagonists is a would-be performer, usually a failure as one, and the unsuccessful performance forms a significant but usually short sequence.

3. The source music is part of the milieu in which the characters appear, either briefly or throughout the film. The bulk of source-music usage in dramatic films fits this category, and the ways in which the music is presented—or can be presented—afford almost limitless possibilities for creative work.

In many dramatic films that cannot by any relaxation of definition be called musicals, examples of the first type occur: the chief protagonist is sometimes a performer, but more often a composer. In a plethora of films produced by Warner Brothers in the 1940s and 1950s, musicians suffered through emotional crises, usually while writing or performing works supplied on the sound track by Erich Wolfgang Korngold. The "suffering musician" has become a dramatic cliché, but at the time the Warner films were released, the characterizations and the accompanying music were acceptable.

There also have been many nonmusicals that were biographies of real musicians. A most notable example is *Song of Love*, (1947) noteworthy musically because of the sound tracks recorded by Artur Rubinstein, but also as a film that, despite its neglect or deprecation by critics, presents

Artur Rubinstein *(left)*, **who played the piano for Katharine Hepburn on the sound track of** *Song of Love*, **with Mrs. Rubinstein and Bronislaw Kaper, musical director of the film.**

Katharine Hepburn in a role that combines her own unique personality with a historical figure, Clara Schumann. The source-music scenes are obligatory in such a film, yet they also add both dramatic as well as musical value. The music played by Hepburn/Rubinstein is, by its nature, highly emotional, typical of the works of Schumann, Brahms, and Liszt.

The Man with the Golden Arm (1956) was an early cinematic treatment of the problems of drug addiction, the leading character being a "mainlining" musician. While drug addiction is not the problem solely of musicians, audiences (and Americans in general) may well have found the linkage of jazz music and drugs a natural one in 1956, and Frank Sinatra's dual identity as musician and addict was an inseparable one. The source-music sequences, with their look and sound of the world of jazz, added an authentic sting to the film's downbeat shock value.

In the films in which the actor (or, more often, the actress) is a would-be performer, such as Susan Alexander in *Citizen Kane* (1941), the failure of the musical performance conveys a development of plot and characterization. The *Citizen Kane* opera sequence is quite short, but that Susan must fail in her attempted career is crucial.

A parallel of the *Citizen Kane* sequence occurs in the 1977 film *Annie Hall*. Annie's nightclub appearance, like Susan Alexander's debut, is a failure: people talk and laugh, dishes and glasses clatter, while she sings "It Had to Be You" (words: Gus Kahn; music: Isham Jones). The "you" is Woody Allen, who displays the same outraged annoyance as Charles Foster Kane, and who tries to cheerlead the applause, much in the manner of Kane. Afterwards, he reassures Annie that she was "great," although she has some doubts about her own talents. Unlike Kane, Allen is not pushing or forcing Annie into an unaspired-to career, but the wistful reactions of Diane Keaton as Annie evoke the same sort of audience sympathy as did Dorothy Comingore in her moment of failure. Thus the sequence and its music function to tell the audience not only what Annie does for a living but, more importantly, how she and Woody Allen relate to each other.

In films in which the chief actors are not musicians, the determining dramatic element—the raison d'être—will have to do with the person's musical leanings or with the milieu itself. The actors may listen to records by choice; they may be at a rock or symphony concert; or they may be a captive audience—in common with the films' actual viewers—in a situation where music, live or recorded, is being performed. This "incidental" but realistic music can actually convey more information than the supposed composition of a fictional composer: it can define or indicate the era of a film, the function of old songs in nostalgia films; reveal the social preferences of the characters, at a piano bar, ballet, or disco; or emphasize their religious ties, as in a John Ford funeral sequence.

In many source-music sequences, the milieu remains important, but the musical elements may be the crucial ones. Like the dramatic elements, the musical ones can elicit an expected response, but often a certain type of music will create a very special and sometimes surprising reaction. Here the primary questions are what type of music is being heard and why, among all the selections of this type, this particular composition was chosen.

There are several ways in which the music itself can be categorized: chronologically, the method used in most texts on music history; by whether it emanates from mechanical reproducers or from live sources; and by whether it is instrumental or vocal, a system usually followed in library classifications. Perhaps the most logical way to classify source music for film-study purposes is according to compositional type, in what must be acknowledged as not in the strictest of musicological terms. The classification system used in this book was chosen with cinematic factors in mind, with primary consideration of what information an individual composition is conveying to the audience.

There are stereotypes in music, as there are in films, and audiences are preconditioned to respond to certain types of music in a certain way. Thus the inclusion of a symphonic work in a motion picture will have a response whether the visuals show someone playing the composition on a phonograph or hearing the work at a concert. With the musical type as a recognized element, the way in which the music is presented is a variable that can be assessed for its effectiveness in a dramatic situation.

A recent example of an often-repeated film scene occurs in *Brothers*(1977). A character, modeled after Angela Davis, is seen in her apartment. She puts a Mozart symphony recording on the record player. This is source music used in its most simplistic form: the audience is obviously supposed to infer, from this action, that this lady has a spiritual (or "highbrow") side to her nature. Part of the ineffectiveness of this scene stems from the fact that it is a cliché, a relic of many previous inclusions in past films.

In *A Clockwork Orange,*(1971) Malcolm MacDowell's love of Beethoven's Ninth Symphony is used for audience response in a most subtle manner; the message to the audience is conveyed in a way that mockingly parallels that of *Brothers*. The irony of the situation is the fact that this "personification of evil" spends his time listening to Beethoven—an echo of the stereotyped usage.

Another example of a constant/variable situation occurs in two different sequences within the same film, *The Heart Is a Lonely Hunter,*(1968). In this film, the same piece of symphonic music evokes a different response with each playing. In an early scene, a Mozart symphony is heard as someone plays it on the phonograph for Alan Arkin. He is a deaf-mute, so it is really the audience, rather than he, that reacts to the *sound* of the music, although he does have a definite response. Later, the same symphony is performed at a concert he attends. This performance produces an entirely different reaction in Arkin. He no longer has the protective one-to-one relationship that he enjoyed when the music was played at home. The large crowd in the hall reinforces his own sense of alienation and isolation.

In the following classification system (Table 1), there are areas in which some music fits overlapping categories, or defies exact classification. The system contains some generalities, in an attempt to avoid confusion of terminology. A large body of music fits the general category of "serious" or "classical" music—i.e., concert music. Such terms have found some disfavor with musicologists or some sector of the music profession. (That jazz has been heard in concert halls and that Beethoven's Fifth Symphony has become a jazz piece are realities that make any system more or less arbitrary.) But the classifications have been selected as the best possible for the analysis of the usages and purposes of source music in motion pictures.

The elements of a specific source-music sequence or scene having been determined, the historian or critic can then approach an analysis of the music and the scene in terms of the filmmaker's rationale and the ways in which he uses music to communicate with the audience.

TABLE 1
Source Music: Compositional Types

I. Concert ("Classical" or "Serious") Music:

    A. Large Orchestral Works
    B. Chamber Music
    C. Virtuoso Solo Instrumental Works
    D. Choral Music
    E. Opera
    F. Ballet
    G. Art Songs and Lieder

II. Nonconcert Music:

    A. Religious Music:
       1. Hymns
       2. Instrumental Works
       3. Choral Works

B. Military Music
C. Jazz and Popular Instrumentals
D. Instrumental Dance Music
E. Folk Songs
F. Popular Songs (including operetta and theater music)
G. Ethnic and Non-Western Music

2
Historical Perspectives of Source Music

While it might be argued that source music originated in the silent film—and certainly pit musicians and theater organists paid careful attention to musical milieus and dance tempos when accompanying the visuals in the silents—its use as a preconceived part of the fictional film began with the inception of the sound era. At various times within that era, source music has assumed varying degrees of importance.

The Jazz Singer, mentioned as the first talkie and the first film in which source music made an important contribution, fits the category of the backstage musical or, more properly, the drama with music. All of its numbers, the religious music and the songs performed by Al Jolson, evolve naturally from the story of the performer who flees his religious ties only to be drawn back to them. "Kol Nidre," which forms the melodramatic climax of the film, emanates directly from the narrative situation. The first *all*-talkie, *Lights of New York* (1928), was a gangster drama, not a musical, but musical numbers performed at the burlesque theater and nightclubs set the moods of the film.

It was not by accident that source music played an important part in these films, and a study of the uses of music in the early days of the sound era provides a clue to the attitudes of producers and filmmakers in general toward film music—and why they often relied on source music for dramatic effects. Those attitudes were largely responsible for the fact that once the movies began to talk, there was very little music in the films except for source music.

The period of transition from the silent film with live orchestral accompaniment in the theater orchestra pit to the period of the all-talking picture was marked first by silent films with recorded music played (on discs) in synchronization with the picture. The first film of this type was *Don Juan,* an amazingly successful picture that opened at the Strand Theater in New York on 6 August 1926. The movie had a recorded score; sound effects of swords clashing were also heard on the Vitaphone records. The score itself, which directly supplanted the pit orchestra, was a harbinger of the eventual elimination of theater orchestras throughout the country. Although the sound tracks had been made to synchronize with the film, perfect sync was not always maintained. A reasonably close proximity to sync was sufficient for audience enjoyment, however.

The Warner Brothers Company followed up the success of *Don Juan* with synchronized scores for subsequent features, including *The Better 'Ole* and *When a Man Loves.* Mordaunt Hall, reviewing the latter film in the *New York Times* on 4 February 1927, describes the film's score and reveals an unusual aspect of the performance:

> *When a Man Loves* was accompanied with a Vitaphone reproduction of an orchestra directed by Henry Hadley. This orchestra effect was so good that there were many in the audience who forgot until the last moment that there were no musicians in the pit. They were reminded of the absence of the orchestra in the pit when the body of musicians was depicted on the screen, and the spectators were moved to applaud.

Just why the studio heads felt impelled to remind that movie audience that there was no pit orchestra, why they exhibited such a self-consciousness, are questions whose answers can only be guessed at. It might have been a gesture of simple acknowledgment. But a more logical explanation is that the Warner Brothers and their associates recognized that there was something artificial in the electronic sound track, an artificiality that audiences would be aware of and possibly resent. From that moment on, it seems, filmmakers believed, just as Hitchcock did, that there was some need to justify the recorded music—an existence whose presence as piano, organ, or full-orchestra music had never been questioned before.

The early days of the sound era also saw a rush to include one or more popular songs or musical production numbers in every picture, musical or nonmusical, on any barely plausible pretext. This trend was partly an outgrowth of the use of theme songs for silent pictures. Theme songs were played by theater orchestras that accompanied the silents, and sales of recordings and sheet music helped stimulate the movies' box-office receipts. The film *Mickey* (1918) was probably the first to have a *title* song (words: Harry Williams; music: Neil Moret) written for it. It was followed by films for which the theme song's title usually represented the name of the feature's heroine: *What Price Glory?*, (words: Lew Pollack) whose "Charmaine" was composed by Erno Rapee, who also contributed the theme of *Seventh Heaven*, "Diane" (words: Lew Pollack). *Seventh Heaven*, a silent film produced just as the transition to sound was beginning, was typical of productions of the time. A sound track of background music and sound effects was added, and at the end of the picture, as the lovers embrace, a coloratura sings "Diane," with full orchestral accompaniment. The vocal continues as exit music after the final fadeout. In later years, theme songs were more often introduced as source music.

By 1928, the movies were filled with talking, singing, and dancing. Films were not yet all-talking, but some thirty-five features contained musical numbers. Yet hardly any of these films would be considered musicals in the traditional sense of the term. Such dramatic films as *Alias Jimmy Valentine*, *Gang War*, *Hit of the Show*, *Laughing Lady*, *Show Folks*, *Stepping High*, *Varsity*, and *Warming Up* (all 1928 except *Laughing Lady* [1929]) contained sequences in which there was source music. Each film featured a song or two, with some sort of excuse furnished for the inclusion.

It was also the beginning of the era of a shot that was to be repeated in countless films: when an excuse for music was needed, someone was seen turning on a phonograph, putting the needle on the record, and listening as the appropriate song or instrumental was heard on the sound track. *Public Enemy* (1931) is an early sound film in which such a scene occurred; there are many more.[6]

A typical example of justified source music in an early film is that described in the *New York Times*, 19 November 1928, in a review of *Gang War:*

> During one scene our little hero, Clyde, undertakes to pass the wee sma' hours playing a saxophone on San Francisco's waterfront. What happens? Just as one might expect. Flowers, the dark damsel impersonated by Olive Borden, chances by and soon Clyde is teaching her to the tune of his sometimes doleful-sounding instrument.

The song featured in the film was "My Suppressed Desire," by Chester Conn and Ned Miller. Its popularity outdistanced that of the film.

In the same year there were films with a show-business background, such as *Hit of the Show*, which featured Joe E. Brown, as a neophyte trying to break into Broadway stardom. There were also films that introduced songs without any obvious reason, such as *Alias Jimmy Valentine*. About the latter film Mordaunt Hall wrote, in the *New York Times*, 16 November 1928: "One may be treated to the love theme song with a scene in which the affectionate couple, Valentine and Rose, are just visible through a wealth of apple blossoms."

They were singing "Love Dreams," which had been composed by William Axt and David Mendoza. Axt and Mendoza had been notable composers of scores for silent films, including *The Big Parade* (1925), *Ben-Hur* (1926), and *Don Juan* and *White Shadows in the South Seas* (1928). They were among the horde of songwriters and theater pit composers and conductors who had migrated from New York to Hollywood when the sound era began.

The first true example of the usage of source music in dramatic film occurs in a picture that was a predecessor of the gangster films that became the trademark of Warner Brothers' action features in the 1930s. The movie is *Lights of New York,* acknowledged as the first all-talking film. It is notable mainly as a kind of museum piece, and apparently its production as a feature was something of an accident.[7]

According to Bryan Foy, director of the film, he conceived the idea that an all-talkie should be made, but had not succeeded in convincing Warner Brothers that such a picture would be saleable. Foy's function at the time of his unsuccessful proposal was the filming of one-reel shorts, and his studio bosses insisted that he continue making them. Shortly after Foy's unacceptable proposal had been made, the Warners left on an extended trip of Europe. They were accompanied by Darryl F. Zanuck, a Warner Studios producer, who also had been mulling over the idea of making an all-talkie. Foy decided that since he made pictures so quickly—shorts were usually completed in a day, and four or five days would be sufficient for a feature—he could easily turn out a feature by the time the Warners and Zanuck returned from Europe.

When the brothers did return to the studio, Foy not only had completed his feature but had interested some exhibitors in it. It was decided to hold a preview of the film at a Glendale theater. As the studio personnel drove up to the theater, they noticed a queue of waiting patrons that stretched around the block.

The film was a success at the preview and at the subsequent engagement at theaters around the country. That the picture *was* a success is more a tribute to the audiences' eagerness for sound than to the quality of the feature. Yet one of the positive attributes of the film was its attempt at realism in portraying the milieu of the underworld. As an example of the use of source music, *Lights of New York* demonstrates how effective the source music could be in conveying not only a feeling of realism, but also the mood of honky-tonk sordidness that pervaded the era of bootleggers and gangsters.

The story of *Lights of New York* is somewhat crudely told, and the necessity of hiding stationary microphones in various places makes for a stiffness in the actions of the cast. Thus whatever realism is achieved is even more remarkable, in a foreshadowing of the best of Warner Brothers' subsequent gangster features. All the musical numbers in the film fit the character of their setting—burlesque theaters and roadhouses. Not so coincidentally, most of the songs heard in the film were from the catalog of the music-publishing firms newly acquired by Warner Brothers, in a move that was emulated by most other Hollywood studios. The fact that the studios owned such catalogs meant that any material from them could be performed in the studios' films without the payment of clearance fees for composers, lyricists, and publishers—while at the same time promoting sheet-music and record sales of the songs in the studios' catalogs. This economy of clearance costs was to become important in the making of both musical and nonmusical features in later years.

By the middle of 1929, the first great surge of film musical production was on. Many of the features being produced were adaptations of Broadway successes: *The Desert Song, Rio Rita, Show Boat, Sally, The Cocoanuts, So Long Letty*, and *Little Johnny Jones*. This was an obvious way to feature stage stars as well as hit songs from Broadway in Hollywood films. There were also many musicals produced from original stories with written-to-order song scores: *Broadway Melody, Gold Diggers of Broadway, Fox Movietone Follies, Hollywood Revue*, and many others. But in other films, production numbers and source music were introduced in ways that added an important dimension to the films.

Applause, produced in 1929, represented an example of the way in which source music could be used for dramatic effect. Many books that deal with the transition period in Hollywood, the early years of sound, have pointed out certain directors who were willing to take chances in pioneering the creative use of sound. Foremost among such people, not only in terms of how often he is mentioned, but because he actually made a substantial contribution, is Rouben Mamoulian. His work in *Applause* is indeed worthy of the many articles and sections of books that have been devoted to it. Yet while historians and critics have been quick to point out that he was using sound creatively, they have somewhat ignored the fact that it was not just sound, but music, with which he—and other noteworthy filmmakers—had been dealing.

The circumstances under which *Applause* was filmed are

Applause: **Helen Morgan on stage.**

important in the evolution of sound films, for they were symptomatic of the problems that had beset the major film companies in the late 1920s. In 1929, in an effort to make filmmaking attractive to stage directors as well as performers from the theater, Paramount had reopened its once-active Astoria Studio on Long Island, after having shut down operations at the facility two years before. Rouben Mamoulian, a young and newly successful Broadway director, had been engaged to direct Helen Morgan, star of stage and nightclubs, in *Applause,* which had been adapted from a novel by Beth Brown. It is a story of a faded actress-dancer, with a background of sleazy theaters and run-down rooming houses. The four numbers further the plot, rather than the story's being an excuse for production numbers.

In several interviews, Mamoulian has described his innovations in sound recording. The most noteworthy is his conception of the idea of using multiple microphones. This technique was necessitated in a sequence in the film in which one microphone picks up the voice of Helen Morgan singing, while another records the voice of her little daughter saying her prayers. The technological importance of that innovation cannot be overstressed. At the same time, however, it is important to realize that Mamoulian was not merely recording two speech tracks; one contained the music. The song that Helen Morgan sings is one that the audience has already heard her performing in the burlesque house. In the prayer scene, Miss Morgan sings it as a lullaby, it being the only song that comes to her mind at the moment. The potential impact of the blending of Helen Morgan's throbbing, throaty singing voice with the thin whisper of a child must have been recognized by Mamoulian. Hence his insistence on recording the two sound tracks simultaneously seems most logical. Viewed—and listened to—today, even in the light of recent technology, this scene from *Applause* is a memorable one.

Rouben Mamoulian has also described the reactions of the Paramount executives who saw the scene in a projec-

tion room soon after it was shot. They immediately gave
Mamoulian permission to continue shooting the motion
picture in any manner he wished, using any technical innovations he deemed necessary, without having to seek
executive clearance.

Throughout the film there are many other scenes that
make use of the theatrical background and its music. It is
the source music that conveys the sense of the pathetic fate
of Miss Morgan, the once acclaimed headliner now fallen
upon hard times. Early in the film, there is a scene in
which the daughter arrives at the burlesque theater where
her mother is performing. A few camera angles are
enough to reveal Helen Morgan's condition, and the
sound of the mother's voice helps convey the shocked sur-
prise in the child's realization of the situation. It is this
shock, of course, which is reinforced for the audience in
the subsequent prayer scene, when the song is repeated.

In *The Celluloid Muse*,[8] Mamoulian mentions that he had
problems with the wardrobe department during the
filming of *Applause:* the costumers kept insisting that Helen Morgan was a star and therefore should be dressed as a
star, not in the dowdy outfits that the director had or-
dered. Whether or not he had similar problems with the
orchestrators, when it came to providing the musical background for the burlesque scenes, has not been documented. But what is heard on the sound track is authentic.
The music has the rhythm and honky-tonk instrumentation of a burlesque house band. At the time the film was
made, Helen Morgan's reputation was not merely that of a
Broadway star; it was that of a *singing* star. There would
have been the added problem of convincing the audience,
which knew her so well, that she was down and out, a has-
been. It is a tribute to her acting ability and to Mamoulian's
directing that the auditory illusion is brought off so successfully. Certainly the musical accompaniment does much
to reinforce that illusion.

Other directors have been cited as pioneers in the art of
making talking pictures, and like Mamoulian's their ef-

Hallelujah: **baptism sequence.**

forts often involved not merely the use of sound, but of music as well. One such director was King Vidor. Among his first sound films was *Hallelujah* (1929). This film is innovative in many ways, one of them being the fact that it was a story of people who at the time of the picture's release were usually referred to as Negroes—particularly in every review of the film. Today, that word has become an anachronism, and perhaps the treatment of blacks within the framework of the movie is anachronistic also. At the time of its release, however, Vidor's treatment of his subject was revolutionary. In terms of the feature's music, both from an artistic standpoint and from a technological one, the film set new standards.

Most of the music is vocal; there is actually very little background scoring. One of the most moving sequences in the film is the baptism scene, in which spirituals accompany the visuals. The sequence also represented one of the first times that postrecording of music was employed. The baptism scene was shot on location, and no sound equipment had been taken along. Careful vocal arranging and synchronization helped make the sequence a highly emotional one.

In other scenes in *Hallelujah*, in dance halls and barrooms, there is evidence that the studio succumbed to the lure of the prospects of a hit song. The two "popular" songs—as opposed to the spirituals—were written by Irving Berlin: "Waiting at the End of the Road" and "Swanee Shuffle." In spite of this artificial interpolation, however, the vocals that are heard throughout the picture enhance the mood and spirit of the protagonists.

Lewis Milestone has also been cited for his work in the early sound film. His most noteworthy effort is *All Quiet on the Western Front* (1929). In it, he utilized somewhat the same technique that Vidor did—the singing of songs without orchestral accompaniment. In the Milestone film, traditional German songs are heard, sung by the soldiers as they march along. Occasionally, they are accompanied by a harmonica. Throughout the film the music evokes a mood—the soldiers' changing attitude toward war—in this earliest of antiwar talkies.

Josef von Sternberg's *The Blue Angel* (1930) cannot be categorized as a musical, even though there is really no background music as such in the film, which is a masterpiece of musical exposition.

The songs that Marlene Dietrich sings at the Blue Angel Café, "Falling in Love Again" (words: Frederick Hollander and Sammy Lerner; music: Frederick Hollander) and "Blonde Woman," have become so closely associated with her and with the film itself that one is almost tempted not to notice how deftly composer Frederick Hollander has utilized source music in various ways throughout the production. The plot concerns the fact that a professor has fallen in love with a nightclub singer, and the opening shots focus on the professor as he whistles a German chorale tune. Then the chiming clock over the gates of the university plays the same tune. At the end of the picture, when the professor dies, muffled chimes are again heard playing the chorale theme.

In *The Blue Angel,* as in many other dramas with music, the chief protagonist is a performer. But in the composition of "Falling in Love Again" Hollander has done more than merely compose a song for Marlene Dietrich to sing: he has created the perfect vehicle for the character she portrays. Thus the source music of the Blue Angel Café scenes functions in the same way that dialogue might—to reveal and establish a character.

Cavalcade, directed by Frank Lloyd and released in 1932, is notable first because it was a very early example of the nostalgia film, and second for its use of source music.

Cavalcade: **Fanny Bridges (Bonita Granville) dances with buskers on a London street.**

The feature won an Academy Award for Best Picture of 1931–32; viewed today, it remains a vehicle of great dramatic intensity.

Cavalcade traces the fortunes of a well-to-do English couple, from the start of the twentieth century until the date of the film's production. Written by Noel Coward, it offers his own commentary on the broad sweep of history that is chronicled. Although there is very little background scoring, the music, almost entirely source music, is important in setting moods and conveying them to the audience. Only one of the film's songs was written by Coward, a distinguished songwriter as well as an actor-playwright, but it is probably his influence that resulted in the inclusion of so much source music on the sound track.

The beginning of the new century is accompanied by toasts and "Auld Lang Syne"; England's involvement in the Boer War, by bands playing "A Soldier of the Queen" and café chorus girls singing recruitment songs. The Maryott family watches the offstage funeral procession of Queen Victoria from the balcony of their home while the dirge being played by the military band becomes louder and louder and then fades away, as the family members' expressions mirror the somberness of the event. The source music helps maintain the illusion. In the sound systems in use at the time of *Cavalcade*'s production, there were no facilities for any stereophonic effects of "pan potting," a technique that makes the sound seem to travel across multiple speakers. But the sensation of moving sound *is* achieved in the film, by a combination of the suggestions of the visuals and minor adjustments to sound levels.

At the end of the mourning period, the Maryotts participate in an elaborate ball, with dancers whirling decorously to Strauss waltzes. In contrast, their servants' child (Bonita Granville) joins a group of buskers dancing to the spirited tunes of a Salvation Army band.

One of the film's major dramatic sequences concerns the sinking of the *Titanic*. An episode such as this has been repeated in so many subsequent films that the original now becomes the cliché. But the shipboard scenes are still evocative: the Maryott son and his bride are on their honeymoon on a luxury line, the identity of which has not been revealed to the audience. They are blissfully happy, as only young English couples could be in 1930s films. Again, the source music sets the tone: Strauss waltzes, in updated arrangements. As the couple walks along the deck, they pass a life preserver bearing the name of the ship, the *Titanic*. The lilting music provides the counterpoint. Today, one can only imagine the impact this revelation must have had on its contemporary audience.

Britain's entry into World War I evokes another change of mood and music: a medley of recruiting songs; Ursula Jeans, the grown-up counterpart of Bonita Granville, dancing in a fashionable café; a montage of marching soldiers, singing "Tipperary" and "Pack Up Your Troubles."

Cavalcade reaches the early 1920s, and the source music is provided by a radio playing the only number actually written for the picture, Noel Coward's lament for the era, "Twentieth Century Blues." The radio grille dissolves into the actual café where Ursula Jeans is singing the song, accompanied by an orchestra of black musicians. The depressing aspects of this sequence are reinforced when the scene shifts back to the Maryotts, toasting the New Year and listening to "Auld Lang Syne" once again. Retrospectively, the couple's optimism seems especially ironic in the light of all that has transpired for England and the rest of the world since 1933, but the couple's hopes for the future also seem a little more lofty for having been so unfulfilled.

Viewed as a vehicle for source music, *Cavalcade* remains an outstanding example. Because the film covers such a long time span, it can be regarded both as a retrospective and as a commentary on contemporary life of its time. The music communicates a sense of the emotional and sociological factors that are involved. "Twentieth Century Blues" is a commentary on an era, a kind of forerunner of the satirical songs of *Cabaret*. The song, like others in *Cavalcade*, represents optimum choice of musical elements.

Cavalcade is also significant because its production came just on the threshold of a change in the format of film music, the beginnings of the era often referred to as the "golden age of Hollywood music." What people really mean when they refer to a golden age of film music is one in which the symphonic background score was predominant and extremely popular. Roger Manvell and John Huntley (who prefer the term "functional music" to "background scoring"), wrote:

> By 1933, the symphonic style of music score for films had begun to be developed. Prokofiev composed one of the first scores in this manner for *Lieutenant Kije* (1934) and Flaherty's *Man of Aran*, with its symphonic score by John Greenwood, was heard in the same year. At Denham Studios, Arthur Bliss was called in to work with Alexander Korda and his Music Director, Muir Mathieson, on Britain's biggest pre-war production, H. G. Wells' *Things to Come*. Simultaneously, Max Steiner was working in Hollywood on the score for *The Informer*. He was also writing for a major symphonic effect—and using a large choir. So, by the end of 1935, two major film scores had appeared, both with "heavenly choir" finales, and both soon to be adapted for concert hall performances and recorded for the gramophone.[9]

Actually, Max Steiner's scores for *Symphony of Six Million*, released in 1932, and *Bird of Paradise* and *King Kong*, released in 1933, had already exhibited some of the characteristics that helped Steiner win the 1935 Academy Award for Best Score for *The Informer*. In 1934, the first year that Academy music awards were given, he had received a nomination for the score of *The Lost Patrol*.[10] About *Symphony of Six Million* Steiner has said:

> Selznick was not satisfied with the result of his filming and said, "Do you think you could put some music be-

hind this thing?" . . . I did as he asked, and he liked it so much he told me to go ahead and do the rest. Music until then had not been used very much for underscoring—the producers were afraid the audience would ask, "Where's the music coming from?" unless they saw an orchestra or a radio or phonograph. But with this picture we proved scoring would work.[11]

As the self-consciousness of the movie producer and studio executive concerning film music seemed to diminish, and the symphonic background score became very much the norm, the rationale of using source music to justify the presence of any music became less and less prevalent.

The era of the symphonic background score did not witness a hiatus in the use of source music in fictional films, but the usage fell into fairly definite and predictable patterns. And an unfortunate side effect of full orchestral scoring was that in many dramas of the 1940s and 1950s the visuals did not match the sound tracks. From old-fashioned gramophone horns and live children's orchestras came the sound of the studio orchestra, as in *Gunga Din* (1939) and *An Affair to Remember* (1957), among many other examples. Church choirs and other amateur groups were in sync with the voices of competent professionals—not always, but far too often.

The visual elements of certain types of films usually made specific types of source music obligatory. Gangster films often had speakeasy, nightclub, and theater sequences. *The Roaring Twenties* (1939)—both a gangster and a nostalgia film—was typical, with its five interpolated "standards" from the Warner Brothers music-publishing catalog. Romantic comedy-dramas usually featured party and café scenes, with appropriate cocktail bar and party pianists and dance bands. The so-called women's pictures, most notably those released by Warners, devoted a great deal of footage to musicians and musical families: *A Stolen Life* (1946), *Deception* (1946), *The Constant Nymph* (1943), which contained original concert compositions; and *Four Daughters* (1938), *Four Wives* (1939), and *Four Mothers* (1940), with chamber-music bits and a composed for the film *Symphony Moderne*. Among individual films, even an epic of the proportions of *Gone with the Wind* (1939) featured a source-music sequence that contrasted neatly with the sweep of battle and burning: the Atlanta bazaar, with the widowed Scarlett waltzing around the dance floor to the shocked disapproval of her peers.

Throughout the sound era, there have been many comedy sequences that involved source music, from pratfalls on the dance floor to Rex Harrison's satirical imitation of Sir Thomas Beecham in *Unfaithfully Yours* (1948). The outstanding example of source-music usage in a comedy occurs in *Love in the Afternoon*, released in 1957.

This film has been the target of adverse criticism in studies of Billy Wilder that have been complimentary to most of the director-writer's other films. It is, however, one of his favorites among his own works. At the third annual Marvin Borowsky Distinguished Lectureship in Screenwriting, held at the Academy's Samuel Goldwyn Theater on 11 April 1977, the film was Wilder's choice for screening. It is, in addition to being a sophisticated and romantic delight, unique in that its source music—and the performance of it—*is* the comedy, and invokes the audience's laughter; yet the source of the laughter is not what is usually called "funny" music.

Love in the Afternoon is the story of a millionaire roué (Gary Cooper) who pursues and is pursued by a naive student (Audrey Hepburn). Part of his seduction technique calls for the services of a quartet of violinists who play "Fascination." Wilder has stated that he remembered hearing "Fascination" played in European cafés; his choice of the number was especially wise. A schmaltzy nightclub gypsy sort of melody, the song itself conveys to the audience an insight into Cooper's personality: this is the sort of music he needs and uses for his rendezvous. At the time of the film's release, the song was probably as unfamiliar to

Love in the Afternoon: **Audrey Hepburn, Gary Cooper, and strolling musicians.**

American audiences as an original composition would have been, and that unfamiliarity was fortuitous. In this case, the performance of a well-known piece would have carried with it too many built-in connotations.

The musicians in the rendezvous scenes of *Love in the Afternoon* are comedy characters, not because of broad mannerisms or funny costumes, but rather because of their impeccable clothes and the businesslike manner in which they go about their musical duties. Like the music itself, they communicate information to the audience: a blasé boredom, probably brought about by having performed their duties for the millionaires too many times—a cynical awareness of the excessive romanticism.

After the release of *Love in the Afternoon,* "Fascination," by F. D. Marchetti and M. de Ferandy, became a hit song in America. Perhaps in time more and more critics will

regard the film with the affection that its director has for
it.

Another perspective of source music during the era of
the symphonic "wall-to-wall" background score can be
viewed by considering the sound-era films of a specific
director, in this case John Ford. Ford maintained a consist-
ent musical style in his sound films that characterized them
as much as his visual autographs.

Ford has said, "Generally, I hate music in pictures—a
little bit now and then, at the end or the start. . . . I don't
like to see a man alone in the desert, dying of thirst, with
the Philadelphia Orchestra behind him."[12]

This is again a manifestation of self-consciousness about
music, and it may be that this feeling is especially prevalent
among people who made the transition from silent films to
talkies, as Ford did. Background scores for his films have
been written by Max Steiner, Alfred Newman, Richard
Hageman, Victor Young, Franz Waxman, Alex North,
and other distinguished composers, but Ford seems more
comfortable in his motion pictures with the inclusion of
band music, square dances, music boxes, buglers, and the
unaccompanied singing of hymns and folk songs.

Salute, released in 1929, set the pattern for later Ford
films. It featured an actual commencement ball, filmed at
Annapolis. In subsequent films, dances of every type became something of a Ford trademark: the dance on the
foundations of the church in *My Darling Clementine* (1946);
the Saturday-night dance in the Hooverville of *The Grapes
of Wrath* (1940), with Henry Fonda singing an awkward,
out-of-tune "Red River Valley"; the killjoy-spoiled officers'
and noncoms' dances of *Fort Apache* (1948).

J. A. Place observes:

The influence of the women in Ford's films is often
shown through dances, which express the unity of the
community through music and movement. Dances are
the warm, human side of cavalry life, the community life
of the army, and the traditional expression of society's
togetherness.[13]

Dances and songs in Ford films also have a diversionary function. They serve as the "calm before the storm," a respite to relieve the tension of conflict and violence.

Ford's direction of *The Informer* won him an Academy Award in 1935; as was mentioned, Max Steiner received an award for his music in the same film. Steiner's haunting background themes did much to sustain the ominous mood of the film. Yet one of the most touching moments occurs when a young boy standing on a street corner sings "The Minstrel Boy," to the accompaniment of an out-of-tune violin. He continues his song as he is searched by the police, and when they offer him a coin for informing, he throws it away without missing a note of the song.

In some Ford films the source-music usage was not so effective and considerably less subtle, the reason for the ineffectiveness being the director's motivation. In *Wagonmaster* (1950) and *Rio Grande* (1950), the Sons of the Pioneers, disguised as cavalrymen, sing many songs, some of them composed for the films. While the situations themselves evoke a nostalgic response, there is something about the Grand Ol' Opry delivery, which is a bit too slick and professional, that cannot be separated from the total communicative effect of these sequences.

How Green Was My Valley, winner of another directorial Academy Award for Ford, and one for best picture, in 1941, is the outstanding example of source-music usage in a Ford film. Like some of his other pictures, this one tells the story of family disintegration, and of the crumbling mining town in which the family lives. There is a moderate amount of background scoring by Alfred Newman, but the bulk of the music consists of Welsh folk songs, sung by the Eisteddfod Singers. A *Time* magazine reviewer wrote of *How Green Was My Valley* (24 November 1941): "For the most part the actors are silent, as befits inarticulate people." They are silent only in terms of speech; these same people are noted for expressing themselves in song, and the scenes of the miners singing as they march home from the mines does not seem the least bit unnatural. Neither do their songs on all sorts of other occasions—weddings, funerals, a performance before royalty—and the songs are interwoven into the plot so as to be an integral part of it. Ford has taken this natural affinity for music of the Welsh people and made it into a seemingly ingenuous means of communicating their emotions.

It must also be noted that in this film the professionalism of the singers is believable and acceptable, as part of a cultural heritage.

Elmer Bernstein, in "What Ever Happened to Great Movie Music?," traces the decline of the symphonic background score in films.[14] He blames the decline on the rise of the hit-record syndrome, the genesis of which he attributes to the title song (by Dimitri Tiomkin) from *High Noon* (1952). Whether or not his hypothesis is valid, the symphonic score did begin to lose favor in the mid-1960s. At the same time jazz scores, whether integrated as source music or used as background, were heard more and more often. There were economic reasons, also, for the elimination of large orchestras and the inclusion of small groups in films.

Amid all these factors, source music assumed a new importance in dramatic films. It once more became a major type of music utilized in film scoring, as part of the old "excuse for music" rationale. Not that background scoring has disappeared; it has even enjoyed a mini-renaissance in films such as *Star Wars* (1977), with its rousing, platinum-record-winning music.

Source music in the films of the late 1960s and 1970s has been very much a reflection of the motivations of its filmmakers. In some cases, the inclusion of music blasting out of radios placed in strategic places has become ludicrous. *Car Wash* is a case in point. It is plausible that the film's music would be heard as incessantly and as pervasively in a real car wash as in the movie. But the exploitation—and success—of the sound-track album implies something beyond cinematic values in the motives of Universal Studios.

But the sixties were marked by some very appealing

inclusions of source music. In *Breakfast at Tiffany's* (1961), Audrey Hepburn strummed a guitar and sang a song that expressed something of her philosophy of life, and "Moon River" (words: Johnny Mercer; music: Henry Mancini) became an all-time movie hit. The use of old songs in such films as *Elmer Gantry* (1960) and *Bonnie and Clyde* (1967)—the former featuring prayer-meeting songs and the latter the voice of Rudy Vallee—prompted the Music Branch of the Academy to change its categorization system in 1961 to include an award for musical adaptation. Nominees *Cat Ballou* (1965) and *A Thousand Clowns* (1965) were noteworthy for their source-music sequences. *They Shoot Horses, Don't They?* (1969), which is discussed in detail in chapter 3, was the decade's best example of the use of old songs in a film.

The 1970s and early 1980s witnessed a great diversity of subject matter and narrative style in motion pictures, as well as an eclecticism of musical treatment. In spite of the doomsday prophets, film background music did not become extinct, and two innovative films, both directed by Bob Fosse—*Cabaret* and *All That Jazz*—gave new promise of how exciting a movie musical can be. Source music was used in a variety of effective ways, often reflecting the multiformity of the features themselves—from the jukebox music of *The Last Picture Show* to the wedding scene of *The Deer Hunter* and the parody of an entertainment of overseas troops in *Apocalypse Now.*

3
Three Special Types of Source Music

Three major types of source music have been selected for study in detail in this chapter: popular songs as performed in the nostalgia film; serious concert and opera music composed for specific motion pictures; and ethnic source music, both ancient and non-Western.

Each of these types presents unique problems for the composer or musical director, problems that have been solved in various ways. In the use of popular songs in a period film, or the performance of ethnic music, one of the major considerations is authenticity. In the case of specially composed compositions, the musical merit of the piece outside the film and the availability of the music for study or public performance become important factors to the music researcher. In none of these subsections has an attempt been made to include all known examples of the type being discussed, but the examples are a representative group in each of the three categories.

Songs in Films of the American Past

America's recent nostalgia craze has extended not only to clothing and interior decoration, but to the motion picture as well. In the profusion of films that cast a backward glance at the life and mores of the United States during

50

the last half-century, there has been an almost mandatory pattern for the sound tracks of these motion pictures: each must contain a sampling of popular songs of the period, in a synthesis of the ways the tunes actually sounded in the age that is being depicted. The music of these films forms a continuum that ranges from the evergreen standards of the 1920s to the ephemeral rock hits of the 1960s, from *The Great Gatsby*'s Jazz Age to *American Graffiti*'s era of the "deuce coupe."

Performed songs in dramatic nonmusical films are informational, telling the audience just when the action is taking place. They can evoke an emotional response, depending on the age range of the audience: a song in a film might have meant something special to the moviegoer ten, twenty, or more years ago, when he or she listened or danced to the same tune. The songs can have a special appeal to those who are too young to remember them, an attractiveness like that of Art Deco furniture and 1920s clothes, that has to do with some longing for a never-never land of perfection that might have existed long ago.

In the many recent nostalgia films that have used source music, the sound track has taken one of two directions. The music can consist of old records of songs that were popular in the period—the method employed in such films as *The Last Picture Show* (1971), *Paper Moon* (1973), and *American Graffiti* (1973)—or the music of a bygone era can be re-created by performing musicians. Examples of careful execution of the latter technique occur in *What's the Matter with Helen?* (1971), *They Shoot Horses, Don't They?*, and *The Great Gatsby*, (1974).

The first method is the simplest. It does away with problems of synchronization and authenticity. If the record has been chosen with reasonable care, authenticity is assured. When the sound coming out of a jukebox in a filmed scene is a Hank Williams record, almost everyone in the audience will know that the movie is set in the 1950s.

The best example of a fairly recent film that made extensive use of phonograph records as source music was

also the first film for which Peter Bogdanovich received
widespread recognition: *The Last Picture Show*. In the film,
Bogdanovich set out to evoke a milieu of a gradually at-
rophying Texas town in the 1950s. He accomplished the
effect visually. He also did it in the sounds of the wind
blowing tumbleweeds through dusty streets, and especially
through the plaintive music that poured out of car radios,
jukeboxes, home phonographs, and television sets.

The film opens almost in silence. Gradually the sound of
the wind becomes audible, as the tumbleweeds roll across
the screen. Then there is the wheeze of an old truck stalling, being revved up, stalling again, and finally starting.
When the engine starts, so does the car radio. Hank Williams's plaintive voice asks, "Why Don't You Believe Me?"
(words and music by Lew Douglas, King Laney, and Roy
Rodde), and the pattern of the sound track has been established.

Having decided that the song records would be the
music in *The Last Picture Show,* Bogdanovich carefully determined the types and the individual selections. He leafed
through every issue of *Billboard* and *Cashbox* published in
1951 and 1952 and compiled a list of two hundred top hits
of the period. He obtained records of these songs and
listened to them all before making the final choices. (Bogdanovich also added his own version of the Alfred Hitchcock touch to the film: he did all the voice-overs represent-
ing the disc jockey.)

Although the film's songs seem to emerge from the
loudspeakers in the most random, haphazard way, actually
they do relate to the action in many of the key scenes. The
most obvious differentiation can be noted in the two diver-
gent styles of songs that are heard. The poolroom jukebox
features Bob Wills and the Texas Playboys, and Hank Williams. It is natural and apparent that Timothy Bottoms
and Jeff Bridges prefer country-western music, as do most
of their friends. Jacy, as played by Cybill Shepherd, and
her boyfriend would rather hear Tony Bennett singing

"Blue Velvet" (words and music by Bernie Wayne and Lee Morris) and other middle-of-the-road numbers.

The party that Cybill Shepherd attends with the new-found wealthy boyfriend, and the striptease into which she is coaxed while balancing on the swimming pool diving board, has a kind of "inside joke" as the musical accompaniment. The record that is played as she disrobes is remindful of a more closely censored era, and the speciousness of that censorship. The song is "The Thing," which achieved great popularity because it was considered "suggestive," an adjective that is rarely applicable in today's "open" society. The song's popularity could be traced more to its innuendos than to what its lyrics actually said: "Get out of here with that ____ ____ ____ [three drum beats] / And don't come back no more."*

There are three segments of the film that feature live source music, in an effective contrast to the sequences that feature recorded songs. One of these, the Christmas dance, with the country-western combo turning out "Red River Valley" and "Jingle Bells," is an excellent complement to the western recordings, reflecting accurately the taste of the townspeople. Two other sequences of necessity called for live music: the high school graduation, with the voices of the students and the amateurish piano accompaniment, and the "big-game" atmosphere of the high school football game, with the school band striving to engender some enthusiasm for underdog Anarene High.

The source-music format of *The Last Picture Show* continues to the end of the film. The reconciliation of Timothy Bottoms and Cloris Leachman is accompanied only by the droning organ and sepulchral voices of a religious radio program. The very last scene again features the sound of the wind blowing through the town, which looks even more desolate than at the beginning. There is

*"The Thing," words and music by Charles R. Grean, © 1950, renewed 1978, by Charles R. Grean, published by Grean Music Co. All rights reserved. Used by permission.

no music. Only during the end titles, which give the complete credits, is the voice of Hank Williams, reprising "Why Don't You Believe Me?," heard again.

In *Paper Moon,* Bogdanovich took another look at America's past, and followed the musical format he had established in *The Last Picture Show* with well-known songs and famous performers of the 1930s. In the more recent movie, the principal source devices are an auto radio and a table radio that Tatum O'Neal carries with her from town to town, plugging it in whenever she and Ryan O'Neal bed down in some rundown hotel or motor court.

Interspersed with the songs that are heard, the radios bring in a couple of old comedy radio shows, too: those of Fibber McGee and Jack Benny, a parallel to the television programs that are heard but only briefly seen in *The Last Picture Show.* The canned music in *Paper Moon* helps to evoke some nostalgic responses to its numerous songs, but the music is not as effective as in the earlier film. One reason is that the audience is too conscious of the famed, distinguished voices, which either have been stilled by death (Dick Powell) or have changed quite radically in timbre (Bing Crosby).[15]

The question of whether the audience should or should not notice film music is one that has been debated for many years. The *Exhibitors Herald,* in an article in its 21 February 1921 issue, quoted David Love, a noted silent house conductor, as stating, "the music should never be noticed above the picture, nor call attention to itself as anything more than a setting for the picture." This may have been the first such comment, but it was certainly not the last. In the case of *Paper Moon,* however, it is not the music that draws attention to itself, but the performers. And unless the performer and his or her performance is the focal point of a scene, these voices out of the past *are* distracting.

Another reason for the ineffectiveness of the music in *Paper Moon* is the fact that presence of the source devices is contrived, and thus justification is only specious. Tom

Milne, in the *Monthly Film Bulletin* for January 1974, asked, "How many cheap cars had radios in the Thirties?" Probably not very many. Such an anachronism in a film that is supposed to be establishing a true milieu of the period is self-defeating.

American Graffiti is another film in which the source music comes from car radios, but in the era of this film everyone's car *did* have a radio, and teenagers' car radios were always on, tuned to a rock station.

American Graffiti presents an endless medley of Top Forty records of the 1960s in what seems, superficially, to be an overall wash of undifferentiated music. Yet the film's music is especially effective and appropriate to the film; it is a shiny veneer very much like the candy-apple spray paint job of a teenager's 1960s coupe, forming a perfect counterpoint and counterpart of the depiction of high school Americana.

Not only do the songs come blasting out of everyone's car radio, but presumably everyone is listening to the same station, the one whose studio is shown toward the end of the film. Most of the numbers are done in typical rock style, but there is a divergence in the actual dates of the songs' composition.[16] The only long sequence without music is the one in which Steve's car is stolen while Terry and Debby make love. The absence of the music emphasizes the loss of the car and its radio.

There are personalized touches concerning the recordings: requests for specific tunes for special girl- and boy-friends; the disc jockey, Wolfman Jack, who becomes an important part of the plot when Curt goes to the radio station to try to arrange a radio message for the girl in the white T-bird.

American Graffiti is a film that has been acclaimed for the visual aspects of its nostalgia—"its gleaming, Techniscoped surfaces fairly crackling with the sights of yesterday."[17] The music tracks help convey the sounds of the '60s. One of the sequences—at the radio station—combines picture and sound with equal facility. The

American Graffiti: **the "sock hop" sequence.**

episode captures not only a slice of the era, but a relatively timeless, ongoing phenomenon of America: the small-town, one-man radio station operation. The tower, the transmitter, the clutter of the studio, even the pile of car-tridged commercials and messages—all accompanied by the omnipresent rock sound—give the moviegoer a true representation of the character of most American AM radio stations of the past several decades.

The sequence at the radio station also emphasizes the total effectiveness of the source music in *American Graffiti,* for it is not just rock music that is so much a part of the teenagers' lives, but radio music. In effect, there is a dou-ble source (and justification) for the music in the film, the radios and "the electronic maestro," Wolfman Jack. And if the selection of songs seemingly had been made at ran-dom, the audience—both within the film and viewing (and hearing) it—knows that this is the way Wolfman Jack has programmed the records.

Save the Tiger (1973) represents a special use of recorded music to establish the mood of a bygone era. The story takes place in the present day, but the leading character, played by Jack Lemmon, is a man whose most pronounced symptom of an impending mental breakdown is the fact that he is living in the past. He talks about Anzio and has hallucinations of World War II's wounded, but he succeeds in transporting himself into the past by playing tape transfers of old records, his favorite being Bunny Berigan's "I Can't Get Started with You" (words: Ira Gershwin; music: Vernon Duke). The recorded songs provide a clue to the magnitude of the impending psychosis, and in its own way the film re-creates another era with the help of the music.

Save the Tiger: **Jack Lemmon listens to an old favorite song being played on the cassette recorder.**

Period pictures that utilize source music that is actually performed by live musicians present a special group of problems for their filmmakers, mainly involving orchestration and synchronization, but the results, both musical and dramatic, can be exceptionally rewarding. There is really nothing very creative about playing a record to accompany a film, even if there is a phonograph or radio on the screen. This criticism is also applicable to the use of records in nonsource background scoring, as in *2001*, *The Exorcist*, and *Barry Lyndon*. One argument against the use of records, particularly orchestral ones such as "Blue Danube" and "Also Sprach Zarathustra," is that they have a frozen, congealed-in-aspic quality; another, that they are a throwback to the clichées of silent theater music, with "tried-and-true" classics from "the old masters." It is unfortunate that *The Exorcist* cannot be screened with the score that Lalo Schifrin wrote for it, which those who attended the film's scoring sessions—before William Friedkin threw out the score and substituted records—praised almost unanimously.[18]

If the source music is to be re-created, the authenticity of the out-of-date orchestral arrangements is an important communicative factor. In the case of period musicals, however, authenticity does not seem to be of importance to the filmmaker. There are musical anachronisms in *Singin' in the Rain* (1952), *Lady Sings the Blues* (1972), *Funny Lady* (1975), *New York, New York* (1977), and *Cabaret* (1972); perhaps the fact that musicals' plots sometimes border on the realm of fantasy, or are secondary to the production numbers, offers something of an explanation. The plot of *Singin' in the Rain*, for example, is historically accurate as far as the problems of the transition of the movies to sound are concerned, but otherwise not very believable. As for the musical numbers that are supposed to be part of the film's parties and movie productions, their orchestrations feature the best, most progressive-sounding work of Conrad Salinger, who, along with Adolph Deutsch, Leo Arnaud, and Calvin Jackson, developed the "MGM" sound of such films as *An American in Paris* (1951), *Band Wagon* (1953),

Gigi (1958), and many others, an orchestral sonority that has enhanced the sound track of *That's Entertainment* (I, 1974; II, 1976) and that does not seem the least bit old-fashioned by contemporary standards. Yet one cannot imagine *Singin' in the Rain* sounding otherwise.

It is in the dramatic period film that re-created source music becomes most important, in terms of both its effects on the audience and the amount of time and effort that must be spent in creating a musical score. Dramatic scenes in which instrumentalists or dancers appear to be performing are usually photographed before the music is added. The matching of instrumentation to picture is one of many problems that require technically skillful musical practice.

What's the Matter with Helen? (1971), a modest-budget film that has become something of a horror classic, is outstanding in its use of re-created source music to establish nostalgia for a bygone era. David Raksin, in a short but carefully postscored sequence featuring child performers, has made clever use of some old Shirley Temple favorites. The episode is set in a facsimile of a 1930s Meglin Kiddie–type talent school, where Debbie Reynolds and Shelley Winters put on a show featuring a bunch of singing, tap-dancing children, none of whom is actually heard on the sound track. In spite of the brevity of the sequence, its camp authenticity makes it the highlight of the movie. The character of this number is closely allied with Shelly Winters's rehearsal piano playing, which accompanies both the dancing school sequences and her final madness that climaxes the drama.[19]

The 1970s often found Hollywood gazing at its own past, mostly in films that viewed the 1930s and 1940s. With one exception, the features were disappointing cinematically as well as musically. That exception is the sleeper *Hearts of the West*, which drew critical praise when it was first released and has slowly built up a loyal following at revival showings. It is unique among films such as *Day of the Locust* and *The Last Tycoon* in that it does not mirror "horrible Hollywood." Rather, the movie cowboys and

Hearts of the West: **the "Pagan Love Song" number.**

backlot workers in *Hearts of the West* show an affection for
the film industry and their Gower Gulch environs, an attitude that was, according to those who were there, the
norm in the days of Mascot Studios and Larry Darmour
Productions.

The music in *Hearts of the West* does a great deal to convey the good-natured retrospection. There is original
background scoring, slightly but appropriately clichéd,
with repeated themes for comedy villains and wild chases.
There is source music, best exemplified in the ludicrous
takeoff of Hollywood production numbers as "natives"
dance to "The Pagan Love Song" (music: Nacio Herb
Brown; lyrics: Arthur Freed) accompanied by what sounds
like an authentic thirties studio orchestra. There are
guitars strummed around the cowboys' campfire. And
there is Nick Lucas (who also appears in *Day of the Locust*)
singing "I'll See You in My Dreams" (music: Isham Jones;

lyrics: Gus Kahn), the tune the young lovers dance to as it comes through that silliest of replicas, Blythe Danner's lamp-shade radio.

There are certain similarities in the way old songs, as source music, have been used in *They Shoot Horses, Don't They?* and *The Great Gatsby,* and music itself has a special sociological connotation in the milieu of each film. *They Shoot Horses'* dance marathon is a means by which victims of the Depression hope to earn a few dollars; the *Gatsby* dance parties are an integral part of the "Lost Generation's" hedonistic pleasures.

They Shoot Horses casts a humorless eye on the dregs of humanity caught up in a 1932 freak show, the dance marathon at a beachfront amusement park in Southern California. Of necessity, there is musical accompaniment for the dancers in almost every scene in the film. In numerous scenes, the camera, mounted on a crane, swings back and forth over the heads of the contestants, bringing the musicians into view at the same time.

All the music for the film except the vocal numbers was postscored by John Green, who served as producer in charge of music, composer, and co-orchestrator, along with arranger Al Woodbury. In an interview,[20] Green stated that planning of the musical score began long before the final shooting script was completed. The producers and money men originally wanted John Green to write a simulated score of "1930s-type" songs, their reasoning being that most young people in the audience wouldn't be familiar with the old songs, that "Johnny Green had done it before and he could do it again," and that it would save clearance costs.

Green refused, he said, believing that such a score wouldn't satisfy the audience, young or old. He won his point, but was told that the clearance budget would be about $26,000. Warning the producers that such a sum would be inadequate to secure the hit songs of the period, Green demanded an "open-ended" budget, telling the backers of the film that the costs would probably be

John Green, associate producer/musical director of *They Shoot Horses, Don't They?*, on the set.

cial musical techniques. There are brief flashforwards as well as flashbacks. In the flashforwards the source music gives way to source underscoring, featuring "Easy Come, Easy Go" in the version that has been heard under the main titles. There are also points in the film where the action is in slow motion: in each of the death scenes—in the *Bonnie and Clyde* tradition—and during the second of the "derbies." The derbies are special events of the dance marathon, grueling footraces designed to eliminate some of the contestants. The second of the derbies begins in a frenzied up-tempo, with trumpet riffs highlighting the arrangement of "California, Here I Come" (words and music by Joseph Meyer, B. G. Sylva, and Al Jolson). Then, as background to the slow motion, the house band, in thumping, limping, 3/4 time, simulates the sound of a carousel, while the contestants seem to be floating through an interminable, excruciating race course. When the motion is back in real time, the frantic music again keeps pace, with the lead saxophonist pacing the group.

Through diversity of instrumentation, through frenzy and lack of sentimentality, the music score and source music successfully match and emphasize the cynicism and depressive atmosphere of *They Shoot Horses, Don't They?* The source music, particularly, is at once informative and evocative.

Whatever the final critical judgment of Jack Clayton's *The Great Gatsby,* its music, among other source-music scores that have been evaluated, is the best and most carefully thought-out example of popular songs used as source music in a motion picture. Musical director Nelson Riddle's contribution to *Gatsby* won for him an Academy Award, one of two Oscars awarded to the much-publicized film. (The other was for costume design.)

Riddle was hired to score the Fitzgerald film after a final cut was assembled and the movie was ready for post-production scoring and dubbing. He was summoned to England late in November 1973 to view the film and begin his work. Five weeks later he was back on the Paramount studio scoring stage in Hollywood, conducting seventy

Nelson Riddle, composer/musical director of *The Great Gatsby*, at work in his studio.

minutes of music he had arranged, adapted, and composed for *Gatsby*.[22]

Riddle spent as much time as possible doing research about music and musical arrangements of the early 1920s. In researching the Jazz Age and scoring *Gatsby*, he faced a problem that had not been encountered by John Green. Whereas Green was *there*, literally, and his own music was very much a part of the era portrayed in *They Shoot Horses*, Nelson Riddle is too young to have more than the vaguest memories of the early 1920s. (Coincidentally, both he and Jack Clayton were born in 1921, so their recollection of *Gatsby*'s era would be somewhat similar.) He mentioned in an interview, however,[23] that his father had been a professional musician, and that the father's band used to practice at the Riddle home when Nelson was a small child. Like

other musicians with total recall, he retained the memory
of that music through the intervening years.

"I think my father's band rehearsed some of the same
songs that are in *Gatsby*," he mentioned. When Nelson Riddle began scoring the film, he tried to re-create that far-
away sound.

Riddle also listened to old records and studied stock
orchestrations, and he found it helpful to study photographs of jazz and popular bands of the period, to learn
what instrumentation they had used. (There are very
few shots in the film itself that make explicit the complement of *Gatsby*'s party orchestras.)

What emerged on the sound track of *Gatsby* is a realistic,
nostalgic, and bittersweet sonority of the West Egg parties,
a happy mélange of muted trumpet fills, the rather hide-
ously authentic triads of three saxophones that only a soprano sax player could love, the wispy "potted-palm"
sound of violins, and the thump of the tuba that reassures
every nostalgia buff that the Fender bass is only an ephemeral fancy.

Yet the overall sound is really more kindly than that of
They Shoot Horses. The arrangements are simpler, less
difficult to play; the melodic lines of the sentimental standards seem mellower, flowing naturally in easy, ingenuous
patterns.

The main titles of *Gatsby* are accompanied by a theme
song, but first there are ghostly echoes of snatches of several old songs, tunes that will be heard later in the film, at
the parties. The theme song, "What'll I Do?" (words and
music by Irving Berlin), is sung in a thin, amateurish voice
(Bill Atherton) that might be that of Gatsby himself. The
mood of the film is set up by the combination of the wistful
theme song and the party-song fragments, which forecast
that the more flamboyant spirit of the age will be depicted.
"There was music from my neighbor's home through the
summer nights."[24] In both the Fitzgerald novel and the
Gatsby film, the dance music is Nick's introduction to Gats-

by's world. In the film, the source music functions much as does the almost constant musical envelopment of *American Graffiti*. A parallel to the sudden silence in *Graffiti* occurs in the final scenes of *Gatsby*, when Nick revisits the now-deserted mansion. The parties and their songs, like the radio and *its* songs, are a part of the life of the protagonists.

Sixteen songs, published between 1917 and 1925, along with two original Riddle tangos, make up the forty-one minutes of *Gatsby* dance-party music. The parties were shot at a mansion in Newport, Rhode Island, where Gatsby's guests danced to guide tracks furnished by Paramount's music department. The songs that are heard in the final version were a combination of the choices of Clayton and Riddle, sometimes—but not always—the same as what was used at the parties. When clearance problems developed over the use of the tangos that were played for the shooting, Riddle wrote two new tangos to match the action of the dancers.

The party numbers were postscored in sync with the guide tracks, and sometimes the dancers themselves served as tempo and rhythmic guides. The numbers represent the truest segment of Americana in the film. Much of *Gatsby* was shot in England, with Jack Clayton's British perspective of 1920s America determining the focus. When it was time to add the music, however, Clayton insisted not only that the composer-arranger be American, but that the music be recorded in Hollywood, with as many veteran jazz and popular musicians as could be hired. The oldest instrumentalist was Jess Stacy, who plays "Beale Street Blues" while Gatsby, Nick, and Meyer Wolfsheim have lunch in a New York restaurant. Stacy had once played in the Fate Marabelle Riverboat Band, which also boasted the talents of Louis Armstrong. But Stacy was a youngster compared to seventy-seven-year-old (in 1975) vocalist Nick Lucas, who sounds as if he really is "Gonna Charleston Back to Charleston" (words and music by Roy

The Great Gatsby: **Mia Farrow, Sam Waterston, and Robert Redford at one of Gatsby's lavish parties. (Photo courtesy of Paramount Pictures)**

Turk and Lou Handman)—if he can get over pining for the days "When You and I Were Seventeen."

In the *Gatsby* party scenes, there were few opportunities to vary the complement of the orchestra. It was assumed that Gatsby had a favorite orchestra—references in the novel point to Paul Whiteman—and the shots of the musicians reveal groups that look, in the fleeting glimpses, similar to each other. Instead of varying the orchestras as a whole, Riddle has let the character and tempo of the songs guide his arrangements: the muted trumpet and trombone of "Whispering" (words and music by John Schonberger, Richard Coburn, and Vincent Rose), the happy hesitations of "The Charleston" (words and music by Cecil Mack and Jimmy Johnson), the accordion and clicking castanets that punctuate the two tangos. Where a different musical group is natural, as in the scenes in a hotel dining room, there is a piano and string ensemble, demurely offering "Alice Blue Gown."

The Great Gatsby also has its "record orchestra," playing at the party in the apartment of Myrtle's friend—"The Sheik of Araby" (words and music by Harry B. Smith, Ted Snyder, and Francis Wheeler), with snake-charmer clarinet turns, and "Yes Sir, That's My Baby" (words: Gus Kahn; music: Walter Donaldson), a Dixieland arrangement. The record orchestra is smaller than the party band, and the strings are almost inaudible.

The film also makes extensive use of source scoring in addition to the straight source music. "What'll I Do?" is not heard as source music until almost two hours of the film have elapsed—as a phonograph record played while Daisy and Gatsby dance by candlelight. The main-title version of the song is source scored. The introduction to the song features plaintive violins and muted trumpets in the style of the 1920s. Then, very gradually, the orchestration shifts to contemporaneous instrumentation. The transition captures the sound and mood of several eras in just a few bars of music.

The theme song is utilized in other music cues throughout the film. In some of them, "What'll I Do?" has been combined with an original countermelody, a technique Nelson Riddle acknowledges as having been used successfully by George Duning in *Picnic,* when he combined the old song "Moonglow" (words and music by Eddie DeLange, Will Hudson, and Irving Mills) with his own "Picnic Theme." The *Gatsby* countermelody is less sentimental than the Irving Berlin tune, but poignant enough to blend well with it as background music.

In the Fitzgerald novel, Klipspringer, the hanger-on, plays the piano and sings a few lines of "Ain't We Got Fun" (words: Gus Kahn and Raymond B. Egan; music: Richard A. Whiting). The scene is duplicated in the film. Over the end-title credits are heard girlish giggles and then two vocal choruses of the song, at once source scoring and Jack Clayton's own commentary on the people of his Jazz Age film.

There are also a few straight background-scoring cues

in *The Great Gatsby,* original material composed for the film. The best is the theme played during the encounter of the illicit lovers, Tom and Myrtle, with a touch of the orchestra color and melodic figurations of Gershwin.

Overall, the score of *The Great Gatsby,* with its blending of source music, source scoring, and background cues, exemplifies just how a period film can be enhanced by its music. The source music's authenticity adds an audibly pleasing aspect to the film, integrity without pedantry.

Asked whether *he* thought it important to be accurate in depicting the past in a film, both in its music and in other aspects, Jack Clayton said, "It's important to me. Whether in the end it's important to the public really isn't my concern. I mean, the last film (the 1949 version of *Gatsby*) was made, and they put it in a different period. If they want to do that, and if nobody minds, that's fine. But as far as I'm concerned, I'm not going to make a film about a classic book, and not have it as near exact as I can get it.

"In *Gatsby,* there are areas where there are so many parties and so much dancing, that the music then becomes genuine music, as though it's going on all about you. And *that* is played and scored exactly as it should have been."

Recent movie releases and schedules of future productions all indicate that motion pictures will continue to look backward at America's past. Indeed, the nostalgia film might well become a true film genre, if it has not already done so. And it is safe to assume that on the sound tracks of these films will be the standards of the 1920s, the "oldies but goodies" of the 1950s, and, eventually, the Top Forty favorites of the 1970s.

Opera and Concert Music Composed for Specific Films

Throughout the sound era, serious works, both operatic and instrumental, have been composed for use as source music in many fictional films. These works can be studied and discussed on two levels: from the standpoint of their function within the film, and as musical entities. In considering the works in the latter category, the availability of the pieces—or the lack of it—must influence the final judgment.

A recent revival of interest in recorded film music has meant that new records of some of the compositions are now available. Some of them have been performed in concerts and recitals, and scores are obtainable from the music publishers. Certain scores are intact and available to scholars in studio or university libraries or in the Library of Congress. But there are scores, unfortunately, that have been lost entirely; not even a sound-track version is available. The compositions discussed in this section have been chosen as representative, and, wherever possible, have been studied in scores.

Opera has been the background for many dramatic films, but the compositional contributions have varied in quality.

The Phantom of the Opera may well be the best-known film *title* having to do with the medium, but much of that fame rests in the silent version, for which David Broekman is credited with having written a special score. But there is no evidence that anything but standard repertoire was played by theater musicians in the appropriate scenes. In 1943 another version was filmed, starring Nelson Eddy and Susanna Foster. It featured a pastiche of synthetic opera selections, written by Edward Ward and based on well-known orchestral themes by Tchaikovsky and Chopin. Ward, a staff composer at both MGM and Universal Studios, succeeded in interweaving such familiar material into acceptable but unexciting music.

In a 1962 version of the *Phantom,* made by Hammer Films, both the background score and an interpolated opera were composed by Edward Astley. The background music is properly menacing, with a discordant, contemporary sound that fits the Hammer treatment of the movie. The opera music, however, sounds stylistically almost exactly like the background music, not only too contemporary for the era in which the action takes place, but lacking in the richness of orchestration that would be necessary for dramatic effect. The lack of contrast also manages to destroy the mood of terror that the background music seeks to establish.

The exact whereabouts of the recent *Phantom* score is not known. Since the earlier (Nelson Eddy) version is based on standard repertoire, it would be available, in orchestral form, in any music library.

Mario Castelnuovo-Tedesco, a composer principally of concert works who wrote occasionally for films, composed two works for operas-within-films that have a great deal of musical merit. One of the compositions worked so well as source music that almost no one has ever listened to it without distractions, however.

The work, a complete aria within an imaginary opera, was performed in *Everybody Does It* (1949), a remake of *Wife, Husband, and Friend* (1939), a Nunnally Johnson production based on a novel by James Cain, *Career in C Major*. The plot concerns a businessman who suddenly discovers he has a superb singing voice. This leads to all sorts of domestic complications and a slapstick opera sequence, the climax of the film. A good deal of worthwhile music is lost in comedy sound effects and the laughter that the film reportedly generated in theater audiences. The sequence reveals Paul Douglas lumbering around the stage in a vaguely Wagnerian costume, complete with breastplate and horned helmet. Careful listening (and reading of the score) does confirm that the music itself is melodic and tastefully orchestrated in a postromantic style. A lyrical soprano aria is performed before the slapstick begins. Both arias could be material for recitals.

A more legitimate performance—and a chance to hear Castelnuovo-Tedesco's music—was given in *Strictly Dishonorable*, (1951). An aria, "Il Ritorno de Cesare," was written for a make-believe opera in which Janet Leigh was called upon to carry the sword of the singing star, Ezio Pinza. The sequence is amusing, but not so hilarious that the audience is unable to hear and appreciate Pinza's robust rendition of the music. The aria is a quartet for mixed voices that combines a virtuoso baritone aria with an interesting but not too intricate orchestral accompaniment.

The aria is available for performance (in conductor's score) from Frank Banyai of United Artists Music Publishing Group, Inc.

One serious work, all but forgotten today, is interesting not only as film source music, but as an indication of some unrealized musical potential of its composer. It is also the longest of operatic "fragments" among so-called opera scores. The work is the opera *Carnival*, written by Oscar Levant for the 1937 production *Charlie Chan at the Opera*. That the film is forgotten does not seem so calamitous; that the music is neglected is more regrettable. As source music, the opera functions routinely in the film. The music itself warrants the close scrutiny.

The entire career of Oscar Levant points to the reality of a great deal of undeveloped talent. Although he attained prominence as a concert pianist, his greatest fame came not as a musician but as a wit and raconteur, as a writer of three popular but now out-of-print books, and as a television and motion picture personality. His work as a composer is definitely full of promise, but little fulfillment. He first tried his hand at writing popular songs, and of the dozens he wrote, one, "Lady Play Your Mandolin" (words: Irving Caesar), became a genuine hit. Another is a sometime favorite of Frank Sinatra and the other singers of middle-of-the-road ballads, "Blame It on My Youth" (words: Edward Heyman).

Levant's serious compositions were mostly written during the period when he was studying with Arnold Schoenberg in Los Angeles. One is a string quartet, of moderate difficulty in performance, but containing moments of restrained yet highly emotional writing. Another is a *Nocturne for Orchestra*, which was premiered at a concert of the Los Angeles WPA Symphony, a concert at which Schoenberg and several of his pupils conducted their compositions. The nocturne has rarely been heard since. It is,

Oscar Levant and his wife, June.

nevertheless, a composition that indicates definite talent that is to be further developed.

Levant's assignment to write an opera for Charlie Chan came about through his employment as a staff composer at Twentieth Century–Fox Studios, in 1937. According to Levant's own account of the state of affairs at the studio, he had not been given any writing assignments, because the head of the music department, Louis Silvers, "was afraid of my jokes."[25] The producer of the Chan series, John Stone, was a friend of Levant's, however. A gentle, quiet man who tolerated the young composer's sometimes eccentric antics and had a respect for his musical talents, Stone arranged for Levant to work on the opera film, along with studio staff composer-orchestrator Charles Maxwell, who was writing background music for the production.

Charlie Chan at the Opera (1937) was a B picture, and although its production values were generally high, there were budget problems. The studio had just completed an expensive film with Metropolitan Opera star Lawrence Tibbett, in which he appeared in a scene from *Faust*. Tibbett had worn an elaborate Mephistopheles costume, which was subsequently assigned to the Charlie Chan picture. Levant summed up one of his compositional problems:

> I've heard of music being written for a singer, but never for a costume. Nevertheless, determined to become a cog in the wheel, I set myself to writing an operatic sequence in which the big aria found a baritone wearing this elegant Mephistopheles costume. As an additional slight detail it was necessary for the aria to work up to a point at which the singer stabbed the girl with a lethal knife malevolently substituted for the prop one. This was the whole point of the picture.[26]

There was no preconceived libretto for *Carnival*. Levant wrote the music first, and then William Kernell, a lyricist also under contract to Twentieth Century, wrote a libretto. Levant states that he never found out just what Kernell had written, because the lyrics were translated into Italian immediately—and sung in that language. (Dual-language lyrics are contained in the score, which is retained in the Twentieth Century–Fox music library, however.)

Levant also states that he had had little experience in writing opera, so he asked Arnold Schoenberg for some advice. "He advised me to study the score of *Fidelio*," states Levant. "Since this is one of the most unoperatic of all operas, it was just what I didn't need."[27]

What Levant wrote is not a complete opera score, but an

overture, a prelude, two marches, and several arias. On some of these segments he shares compositional credit with Charles Maxwell. All of the material that was recorded in the film is retained in the Twentieth Century–Fox music department library, in a conductor's score (three-stave). Copies of all the compositions, in sketch form or in piano reductions, are also in the library of Mrs. Sybil Maxwell, widow of Charles Maxwell. (Mrs. Maxwell also has retained copies of most of her husband's numerous film scores.)

The rather slim score is used generously throughout *Charlie Chan at the Opera,* with repetitions of most of the material. The music that is heard over the main-title credits is the "Baritone Aria," in instrumental form. This aria, called "Then Farewell," is, in the words of Levant, "a potent mingling of Moussorgsky and pure Levant."[28] The Moussorgsky influence is evident in the ponderous bass chords that characterize the opening bars of the introduction, chords that are repeated (in the vocal arrangement) in each statement by the singer. Against these chords the "pure Levant" emerges, but it is really Levant very much under the influence of George Gershwin. Levant utilizes a figure reminiscent of Gershwin rhythms, scored for high instruments—violins and flutes.

After two short cues from the Twentieth Century library, heard behind newspaper inserts, and a piano solo written by Samuel Kaylin and played (dubbed) by Boris Karloff, an instrumental version of "Then Farewell" is heard again, as the "supers" line up and the opera is about to begin. More library music (by Peter Brunelli) is heard, and then the "Carnival Prelude" introduces the opening of the opera.

There is some question about the credits for the prelude. The official credit, on the Twentieth Century score, reads, "Composed and arranged by Charles Maxwell; themes by Oscar Levant." But the credit on the "Carnival Interlude," which is part of the prelude, reads, "Composer, Oscar Levant," and much of the material in the prelude proper consists of measures from the interlude.

The form of the entire composition is prelude/interlude/prelude/interlude/prelude, or ABABA.

No matter who wrote which measures of the complete composition, it is an interesting mélange of alternating rhythmic patterns and striking harmonic usage. The composition is in 6/8 time. One rhythmic figure features a ♪ ♫♫ ♫ pattern. In another figure, sixteenth-note triplets predominate. In a third, the figure is ♪ ♫ ♪, with the figure repeated within the bar. Against these rhythmic figures, the prelude opens with a four-bar cantabile introduction. A two-bar bridge, incorporating a martial motif, leads into a cantabile, ascending within each measure. Then there is another rhythmic section, six bars long. This sort of alternation continues throughout the prelude-interlude.

Musicians, some of them contemporaries and former colleagues of Oscar Levant, when discussing *Carnival*—and the opera is discussed occasionally—most frequently recall the march from *Charlie Chan at the Opera* as the most notable part of the score. Composer David Raksin can still, some forty-five years after the film's release, sing the melody of the composition. It is indeed a musical gem, waiting for rediscovery, reorchestration, and perhaps expansion of its scant twenty-five measures.

The nucleus of the march is a seven-bar theme, characterized by a sixteenth-note triplet figure, an angular yet graceful melody, and some unexpected and provocative chord progressions that revolve around a definite tonality, that of D Major. The theme is repeated with a one-bar extension. After the repetition of the melody, there is a three-bar coda, a fanfare with triplets.

There is a suggestion in the Charles Maxwell manuscript of the way in which the march, as heard in the film, probably evolved. The composition begins with the three-bar fanfare, identical to the one heard at the end. In the Maxwell manuscript, the opening bars are numbered 9–10–11; the same digits enumerate the last three measures of his sketch. Next there is a four-bar phrase, with a triplet figure in the inner voices, identical to the four measures that precede the coda. This is actually the last half of the theme, plus the added bar, and the Maxwell manuscript's numbers 5–6–7–8. Bar 8, at which the theme is heard from the beginning, is numbered bar 1 by Maxwell, and he follows this enumeration to the end of the manuscript. Thus it would seem that the opening seven bars, which serve to introduce the inner-voice triplet figure, are a juxtaposition conceived by Charles Maxwell. Yet, however the overall form of the march may have been altered or the final form arrived at, the march remains a classic of film scoring and of potential concert material. (Table 2 shows the numbering of sketch and score.)

As *Charlie Chan at the Opera* continues and the first scenes on the stage are shown, more music from the Fox library is heard: a long and very dramatic piece by Peter Brunelli, from the score of *Dante's Inferno* (1935). During the playing, an offstage shot is heard.

In the next stage scene the soprano sings "Ah, Romantic Love Dream." In writing about the *Chan* score, Oscar Levant states:

> There were a few turns of phrase which I considered individual, also a harmonic idiom a little more adventurous than that commonly encountered in such writing. It was acceptable to the producers (they liked the soprano aria particularly because it had a good tune).[29]

While the melody of the aria would hardly be appropriate for a popular song, it consists of several lyrically expressive fragments, and is melodically more engaging than the baritone aria.

After a fairly straightforward four-measure introduction, the aria begins. It is "sung" by Boris Karloff, and dubbed by Rico Ricardi. It is thirty-nine bars long. The opening section is really introductory to the andante section that follows. The andante section is basically in A: BA form, which is found in many songs. A two-measure motivic device, including a descending tritone (an interval of a diminished fifth, F natural to B natural) is heard at the

TABLE 2
Corresponding Numbering of Twentieth Century–Fox Score
and Charles Maxwell Sketch for the March from *Carnival*

	Studio Version	Maxwell Version	
	1	9	
	2	10	
	3	11	
	4	5	
	6	7	
	7	8	
	8	1	
	9	2	
	10	3	
* theme	11	4	
	12	—	
	13	—	
	14	—	Not numbered
	15	—	
	16	2	
	17	3	
	18	4	
	19	5	
	20	6	
	21	7	
	22	8	
	23	9	
	24	10	
	25	11	

*The theme is repeated in bars
15–21 of the studio score.

beginning of the andante section and in its closing measures. Most of the melodic fragments are chordal.

In one paragraph of *A Smattering of Ignorance*,[30] Levant characterizes the English lyrics of *Carnival* as "silly." In the case of the words found in the score of "Ah, Romantic Love Dream," that complaint seems justified, or the lyrics might better be described as trite; certainly they do not measure up to the effort that the composer was obviously making to write something that not only would fit the movie, but would be a credit to his teacher, Arnold Schoenberg. The addition of a new set of lyrics (or perhaps a reversion to those in Italian) would make the soprano aria a worthwhile recital composition.

Later in the film, the baritone aria—which is actually a duet—called "Then Farewell," is performed vocally. Rico Ricardi again sings the baritone solo, dubbing for Boris Karloff.

Throughout the opera, Levant has followed the style of his mentor, and has not used key signatures. The baritone aria has a definite tonality, however. The introduction begins in E-flat Minor. It is in 4/4 time. The key remains for two bars, at which point a triplet figure is introduced and the key changes. This triplet figure, with slight variations, is repeated throughout the opening statement of the baritone (bars 12–21).

Next the soprano replies. The meter is now 3/4. Instead of triplets, Levant uses another Gershwinesque rhythmic figure. These alternations of meter continue throughout the duet, which is eighty-five measures long. The overall effect of the shifting chordal figures, jazzlike rhythms, and metric changes is one of agitation and conflict. This is exactly the thrust of the message in the lyrics, at least as they appear in English. In spite of Levant's criticism of the actual words, there is, in the baritone aria, a very good blending of the music and the spirit of the libretto.

A "Marche Funebre," written by Levant, follows a death scene in the film. The march is very short—only six bars were recorded for the film—but it is appropriately morose.

Another aria, "King and Country Call," follows. The solo for baritone (also sung by Ricardi) is noteworthy because of Levant's anecdote about it: he had asked that the word *silencio* be used at some point in the opera. The aria does begin with the favorite word, as "sung" by Boris Karloff, wearing the Mephistopheles costume.[31] After the aria, seventeen bars long, there is a reprise of the Marche Funebre.

The rest of the opera consists of repetitions of some of the operatic material heard before, plus some stock music and a song by Lew Pollack and William Kernell, "Our Little Girl," which Karloff plays on the piano.

In addition to the fact that *Carnival* was performed in an obscure motion picture, there is another reason that it is largely forgotten, one that is important in the consideration of the composition as source music: it is really incidental to the plot of *Charlie Chan at the Opera*, rather than essential to it. The Charlie Chan series films were made according to a formula, with one of the variables in that formula being the location. Many titles in the series are indicative of this factor: *Charlie Chan at the Circus, Charlie Chan at the Race Track, Charlie Chan at Monte Carlo, Charlie Chan at Treasure Island.* Most of the films had either the word *at* or *in* in the title. The opera house was merely one more place for Charlie to visit, in the course of which visit he solved a mystery. Inevitably, such a device becomes worn, and everything connected with it, even a very creditable opera, is just part of a cliché.

But whatever the ultimate fate of Oscar Levant's music for *Charlie Chan at the Opera*, it remains for the time a fragment from an inconsistent but sometimes brilliant career.

In contrast to the anonymity of a film such as *Charlie Chan* and its score is *Citizen Kane* and the opera sequence written by Bernard Herrmann for the motion picture. Herrmann's *Salammbô* is undoubtedly the best-known source-music composition written for a film, and *Citizen Kane* is one of the classics of the American cinema. Unlike the circumstances of the *Chan* opera, Herrmann's work and Susan Alexander's operatic career are essentials of the plot.

The opera has also been the cause of a tempest in a teapot over its origins, the controversy being part of a larger vendetta between Pauline Kael and Peter Bog-danovich about the relative contributions of Orson Welles and Herman Mankiewicz to the picture. In *The Citizen Kane Book*, Miss Kael presents her theory about the reason for the use of an original opera rather than something from the standard repertoire, basing it, as she does most of the material in the book, on a viewpoint that favors Mankiewicz over his co-scriptwriter-director.[32]

The opera sequence occurs in the part of *Kane* dealing with the efforts of Kane to push Susan Alexander's career to its limits and beyond, and to promote her operatic debut. According to Miss Kael, there were strong reasons that *Thaïs* by Massenet would have been a logical choice as the vehicle for these scenes. One is the fact that Mankiewicz refers to the debut opera as *Thaïs* in his original script. Then, in a long and complex explanation of why opera is a proper subject of and target for the barbs of American satirical comedy, she relates this to the fact that Mankiewicz had been one of the original writers assigned to the Marx Brothers' *A Night at the Opera*, but had later been fired from the film. *A Night at the Opera* was a film that had one sequence that made fun of opera, and she somehow implies that Mankiewicz was at last getting some sort of revenge by his treatment of the medium in *Kane*.

She further states that the inclusion of *Thaïs* would have been a reference to the fact that at one time a San Francisco singer, Sybil Sanderson, had been engaged to William Randolph Hearst. To break up the engagement, her parents had sent her to study in Paris, where she became well known not only in opera but as the "constant companion" of composer Massenet. Massenet dedicated the opera *Thaïs* to her, and had, presumably, written it for her to sing.

Miss Kael's final part of her theory is that the use of *Thaïs* would have necessitated paying a clearance fee, and "so Bernard Herrmann wrote choice excerpts of a fake French-Oriental opera, 'Salammbô.' "[33]

All of this theory is quite convincingly shattered by Bernard Herrmann in an interview in *Sight and Sound* (Spring 1972), and by Peter Bogdanovich, who quotes Herrmann in an *Esquire* article, "The Kane Mutiny" (October 1972).

The format of the interview article in *Sight and Sound* alternates quotes from the Kael book with comments by Bernard Herrmann and George Coulouris on the statements. On the subject of Miss Kael's statement about the opera and clearance cost, Herrmann states:

> Pauline Kael was never in touch with me when the book was being written. The musical information is rubbish. . . . She's trying to say that after bringing all these people to Hollywood and paying them salaries for months, they couldn't have paid a modest fee for *Thaïs.* The truth is that no music in *Thaïs* or any other opera would create the impact of that scene—a terrified girl lost in the quicksand of a powerful orchestra. The orchestra plays for forty seconds to develop a tremendous tension before she sings. It has nothing to do with the Marx Brothers.

Not content with such conclusive evidence, Bogdanovich, in his article, quotes a telegram sent by Orson Welles to Bernard Herrmann on 18 July 1940:

> "Opera sequence is early in shooting so must have fully orchestrated recorded track before shooting. Susie sings as curtain goes up in first act, and I believe there is no opera of importance where soprano leads with chin like this. Therefore I suggest that it be original . . . by you . . . parody on typical Mary Garden vehicle . . . suggest Salammbô which gives us phony production scene of ancient Rome and Carthage, and Susie can dress like grand opera neoclassic courtesan. . . . Here is the chance for you to do something witty and amusing— and now is the time for you to do it. I love you dearly. Orson."

But the whole controversy—which does indeed seem trivial when one considers the excellent music that evolved—must be laid to rest forever by the liner notes written by Christopher Palmer for the record album *Citi-*

zen Kane, released in 1974. Palmer enjoyed a close personal and professional relationship with Bernard Herrmann during the composer's last years, and published several interview articles about him during a period when Herrmann was refusing to talk to most interviewers.

The *Citizen Kane* album is noteworthy for bringing to record listeners the vocal selections from *Salammbô,* not as they were sung by Jean Forward, a professional singer who made herself sound like a straining amateur, but by Kiri Te Kanawa, whose brilliant coloratura gives a new depth of drama to the recitative and aria. She is accompanied by the National Philharmonic Orchestra, conducted by Charles Gerhardt, who has also conducted several recent recordings of well-known film scores.

About *Salammbô,* Christopher Palmer states:

> The musical handling of Susan Alexander Kane's debut as an opera singer posed a special problem. Herrmann had somehow to find a fragment of grand opera that would convincingly demonstrate that while Susan possessed a voice of a kind, it was not that of a great opera singer. . . . At the same time this "realistic" music had to serve as a kind of commentary on the action. . . . Herrmann realized that no excerpt from the standard repertoire could satisfactorily fulfill all these requirements. His solution gives us one of film music's most unusual and memorable excerpts, a recitative and aria. . . . The vocal line is consistently high, the orchestral accompaniment so full that only a powerful soprano with a strong top octave could do it justice. . . . For the film Herrmann engaged a light lyric soprano, her best efforts proving so unavailing against the Straussian power of the orchestra as to give the impression that she was floundering in quicksand.[34]

The entire score of *Citizen Kane* is filled with music cues that are examples of source music used most deftly, particularly the "Charlie Kane" number performed at the stag party and later used as a campaign song, the blues background at the El Rancho Nightclub, and the performance of the black musicians who entertain at one of the picnics at Xanadu. But the opera sequence is especially effective, achieving its dramatic impact in just a few moments.

There are only two short scenes, plus a montage, in which the Herrmann opera fragment is heard: one during a rehearsal for Susan's debut, when the camera swings into the rafters to reveal two stagehands, one of whom gives his silent nose-holding appraisal of her singing; another, with almost identical shots, as she performs before an audience, while Charles Kane chafes at the whisperings and derogatory remarks that are being made. (In between is another source-music sequence when Susan sings "Una voce poco fa" from Rossini's *The Barber of Seville,* and her vocal coach, Matiste, tries to resign from the hopeless job.) The opera music is also heard, very faintly, almost as an echo, in the scene in which Kane visits Susan's bedside after her attempted suicide. Then the echoes give way to the ominous chords that accompany the shots of the towers of Xanadu.

Given the task of writing an opera that opens with a soprano solo—somewhat a parallel to Oscar Levant's task of writing an opera to fit a costume—Herrmann could, conceivably, have written just about anything to fit that situation. The most fortunate thing about the resultant music is that given so much leeway, Herrmann wrote something so well conceived and appropriate. Depending upon one's empathies toward Susan and Charles Foster Kane, one can laugh at the fact that Herrmann has provided the "something witty and amusing" that Welles had requested, but it is a cruel and sad joke that touches the emotion of the audience.

The opera fragment is overpowering in its sound of doomsday foreboding—very much in character with the main-title music and that of other sequences—Wagnerian in its low string tremolos and crashing cymbals, in its full brass chords, in the plaintive, almost wailing quality of the soprano's notes. There is even a stylistic suggestion of Richard Strauss, whose own *Salome* fits into the rather loose term *Oriental,* in the full postromantic orchestration of *Salammbô.*

In this context, some consideration should be given to

the term *Franco-Oriental,* as it has been used in the previously mentioned critiques of Pauline Kael, Peter Bogdanovich, Christopher Palmer, and Charles Higham.[35] The term relates to the influence of the Far East at the end of the nineteenth century, an era when the Orient could mean India, Turkey, Egypt, Persia, Africa, or even ancient Greece and Rome. The settings of Massenet's *The King of Lahore* and *Herodiade,* of *Aïda, Lakmé, Salome,* even the earlier productions of *Salammbô,* reinforce this idea. Grout, in *A Short History of Opera,* uses the terms *orientalism* and *exoticism* interchangeably.[36] The latter term, however, seems more properly descriptive.

The entire score of *Citizen Kane,* including the opera, has been placed in the Library of Congress. In addition to the opera aria, several other portions of the film score have been recorded.

Concert works composed as source music for specific films differ in several ways from operatic pieces written for similar usage:

1. The orchestral work is usually supposed to have been written by one of the protagonists in the film; for some unexplained reason, composers in fictional films seldom write operas.

2. There is a greater range of possibilities of form in the cinematic orchestral work than in the operatic composition.

3. The instrumental work is often of substantial length, while the opera selections are usually quite short, consisting of one or occasionally two arias.

4. The orchestral work is often performed in its entirety, or in a slightly cut form; even the short opera pieces are frequently just fragments of the intended aria.

As the creation of one of the protagonists in a film, the source-music symphony, concerto, or rhapsody assumes an importance as a statement about the personality of the imaginary composer. The style of the work is a reflection of his (or her) own emotional life-style, or ideals and aspirations. Generally, these musical compositions are written in romantic or postromantic styles, emulating Tchaikovsky or Rachmaninoff in piano works, and often have an "uplifting" character in the climaxes.

A film musical affords songwriters the opportunity to introduce new material into the popular-song field; the dramatic or comedy motion picture with a musical background would seem to afford the same sort of opportunity for composers to write new concert compositions for the repertoire. A few of these works have later been heard in concert programs, but on the whole they have been unpublished, unperformed, and forgotten, without a life outside the film.

One exception to this sort of oblivion is the *Warsaw Concerto,* which was heard in an English production, *Suicide Squadron.* Released in 1940 (1942 in the United States), the film is the story of a Polish pianist who joins the RAF during World War II. One sequence called for him to play a portion of a concerto, composed in the style of Rachmaninoff.[37] Richard Addinsell produced what Muir Mathieson, music director of the movie, described as a "nine-minute tabloid concerto."[38] No credit was given the work in the titles, but when the film opened in London, the studio began to get inquiries about the music. A commercial record, taken from an outtake of the music sound tracks, was released and became an almost-overnight bestseller. Copies of the sheet music sold with equal success. The composition soon became a favorite in "pops" concerts and as a piece for aspiring young pianists, almost replacing *Rhapsody in Blue* as a showcase for young virtuosos at recitals and high school graduations. *Warsaw Concerto*'s peak of popularity having been reached in the mid-1940s, it became a "standard," slightly less well known, but today it is still a staple of appearances by such pianists as Peter Nero and Roger Williams. Published in several different versions, it enjoys healthy sales, particularly in an edition for piano solo, according to David Jacobs, Chappell Music Company executive.

The atmosphere most conducive to the writing of "clas-

sical" music for films, in the 1930s and 1940s, was that at
Warner Brothers. The exact reason for the proliferation
of serious compositions is not known, but certainly it can
be attributed to the fact that such composers as Max
Steiner and Erich Korngold were under contract there for
many years, and to the general attitude of the executive of
the studio, Jack Warner. A longtime musical director at
that studio has said that Warner once told him he would
like the music to begin when the Warner logo came on,
and to end when the picture said, "The End." "Wall-to-
wall" scoring was the norm in most Warner films of those
years.

The earliest composed-for-the-film opus is *Symphony
Moderne*, played as a theme in *Four Daughters* (1938) and
performed by a full symphony orchestra in *Four Wives*
(1939). *Four Daughters* was based on a magazine story by
Fannie Hurst that dealt with the lives and loves of a music
professor and his attractive young daughters. The studio
had bought the story, and screenwriters Philip Epstein and
Lenore Coffee had added to the cast the character of a
young pianist who comes to live with the family, a cynical,
angry rebel who characterizes his composition—and by
implication, life itself—by saying, "It stinks!" The role was
played by John Garfield, in his first featured screen part.
Garfield based his appearance and mannerisms on Oscar
Levant, although the characterization was one of intense
seriousness rather than the wry impudence of Levant in
real life. Garfield's performance deservedly won him almost instant success. "Mickey's Theme," the target of his
self-criticism, which Garfield plays at the piano several
times, becomes background music, scored for full orchestra, as the story becomes more melodramatic.

The theme itself is very much in character with the personality of Mickey—nostalgic without sentimentality,
rhapsodic, the sort of thing a young composer might be
writing in the 1930s, or beginning to write and not quite
finishing. It fulfilled the requirement of being music that
the audience could believe Mickey Borden would write.
Without detracting from John Garfield's acting ability,

Erich Wolfgang Korngold instructs actor Alan Badel, playing Richard Wagner in *The Magic Fire*, in the art of conducting. (Photo from the Korngold Collection)

some measure of his instantaneous popularity must be attributed to the music he "composed" for the film, and to Max Steiner's development of the theme into rich background music, not unlike that of *Casablanca*.[39]

Because of the nature of the stories, all of the "Four" series—*Daughters, Wives, Mothers*—had numerous source-music sequences. In the second film, *Four Wives*, Jeffrey Lynn, the friend of John Garfield, who died in the previous film, writes an expanded version of the "Mickey Theme," called *Symphony Moderne*, and it is performed by a symphony orchestra. (The piece was written by Max Steiner and Max Rabinowitsh.) Something of the impact of the composition had been lost, however, perhaps with the disappearance (except in a flashback) of Garfield from the series, and the blending of music and characterization is never quite captured again in the rest of the family chronicle.

Symphony Moderne was published by Warner Brothers Music Company, but is out of print at the present time.

Composer Erich Wolfgang Korngold has had more chances than any other screen composer to write concert compositions for the films he scored. All of the films in which these works were performed were highly dramatic; none was a musical. But each film had a plot in which fictional musicians were involved in highly emotional situations. And because Korngold, who has been called "the last of the romantic film composers," had a special talent for the melodic phrase and lush harmonic structure—even more than his colleague, Max Steiner—he seemed especially in his element in both background and source music for such films as *The Constant Nymph, Escape Me Never, Between Two Worlds,* and *Deception.*

The Constant Nymph (1943) told the bittersweet story of composer Charles Boyer, who marries socialite Alexis Smith rather than the young girl from a musical family, Joan Fontaine, who loves him and inspires him. Korngold, who was already one of Warner Brothers' star composers, was asked to help with the dialogue of the film, according to Isabel Morse Jones, music critic of the *Los Angeles Times.* In the 18 July 1943 issue, she states: "The composer-hero Boyer does not utter musical trivialities. He talks sense. A serious composer would naturally discuss music as he does in this picture."

Today, much of that dialogue seems a bit stilted. But the film gives a more realistic glimpse of musicians than that furnished in most 1940s films. The music that Korngold wrote for the climax of *The Constant Nymph* holds up as an example of the best of "the golden age of Hollywood music."

The composition is a tone poem for symphonic orchestra, solo contralto, and women's chorus. Throughout the film it is heard in various forms, as Boyer works on it: first as a song, then in a fairly dissonant "modern" version, and then in its final form as it is played at a concert of Boyer's music. The last six and one-half minutes of *The Constant Nymph* are given over to the uninterrupted performance. The style is unmistakably Korngold's—richly orchestrated, melodic, with an upbeat, "inspirational" closing that must have had contemporary audiences wiping a tear and applauding "The End."

Escape Me Never (filmed in 1943, released in 1947) was based on a novel by Margaret Kennedy, who had also written *The Constant Nymph,* and the story is also that of a composer. *Escape Me Never* is a film not especially noted for plot, direction, or acting. Its main redeeming feature is its Korngold score. That score includes a ballet written by the composer, played by Errol Flynn. Movie audiences never accepted Flynn in this role, but no one can deny the quality of the music for which the fictional composer is credited. Even before the short performance of the ballet—in a rehearsal scene that is interrupted by an outburst by the ballerina—the ballet themes underscore the emotional conflict of Flynn as he vacillates between loyalty to the devoted Ida Lupino and attachment to the distracting "other woman," Eleanor Parker. This is source scoring, in advance of the source music itself. We never see Errol Flynn "composing," and he plays the piano only briefly, in a party sequence where he performs for an admiring group. The ballet rehearsal scene is the musical highlight of the film, so engaging is the melodic emotionalism and harmonic richness of Korngold's music. "Primavera" is danced by George Zorotch, Milada Mladova, and Betty Bryson. Miss Bryson's husband, LeRoy Prinz, choreographed the sequence.

Between Two Worlds (1944), an adaptation of the play *Outward Bound,* told the story of a group of dead people being transported to the next world. Korngold's son, George Korngold, has said that the mysticism of the plot especially appealed to his father, and that the score he wrote for the film was his favorite of his own motion picture work.[40]

In the film, Paul Henreid plays the part of a concert pianist who attempts suicide. Afterwards, he makes several tortured attempts to play again but is unable to. Finally, he

On the set of *Deception*, Erich Wolfgang Korngold discusses the film's music with Paul Henreid and Bette Davis. (Photo from the Korngold Collection)

walks to the shipboard piano and, with steady hands, plays a short rhapsody that Korngold had composed for the scene. Korngold did the actual playing for Henreid, and the rhapsody is a pensive piece, quite in keeping with the scene.

Deception (1946) was the last original film score by Korngold, although he arranged, supervised, and conducted the music in *The Magic Fire*, a biography of Richard Wagner, in 1954. In *Deception*, the story concerned the triangle of a composer-conductor, Claude Rains, a pianist, Bette Davis, and a cellist, Paul Henreid, and was based on a play, Louis Verneuill's *Jealousy*, originally a vehicle for only two characters, and later a film starring Jeanne Eagels and Anthony Bushnell. The *New Yorker* critic's review of *Deception,* 26 October 1946, stated: "The picture is as handsome a creation as I've seen in a long while, and it's too bad the story is so foolish. You'll hear some fine music, anyway, if you happen upon this one."

Deception is a kind of soap opera, but musically it is of interest, both because of the inclusion of several works from the standard concert repertoire and because Korngold's music is a departure from his own style, containing very little background music but featuring an original cello concerto. The concerto is crucial to the plot. It is a work that Rains, an egocentric as well as eccentric man, has written for Henreid to perform. It again has the quality of sounding like something the character would have written, rather than a typical Korngold composition. Perhaps it is its quality of slight dissonance, severity, and lack of romanticism that has caused Charles Higham and Joel Greenberg to describe it as "hideous."[41] It is not hideous, but it is an interesting virtuoso piece of substance.

For the film recording, the solo part was played by Eleanor Aller Slatkin, and parts of its single three-part movement are heard throughout the film. At first small excerpts are played on the piano by Rains, with Korngold doubling for him; in a rehearsal scene, a middle adagio section is performed. In the climactic finale, the first allegro section segues into the closing fugato.

Korngold later expanded the concerto slightly to form a complete concert work, Opus 37. It has been performed in concerts, is published in Germany by Schott and Company, and has been recorded, along with other Korngold film excerpts, including "Tomorrow," the tone poem from *The Constant Nymph.*

Cinematically, the four Korngold concert source-music compositions function well within each film, as statements of each fictional composer and as part of motion picture music's "golden age" souvenirs. As concert works, the pieces give promise of having an independent life of their own.

In an article that presents a review of Korngold's nonfilm compositions and concert conducting activities, as well as an evaluation of Opus 37, British musicologist S. S.

Dale says of the concerto: "It is surprising that the work has never been publicly performed in England. Here is a chance for some cellist who does not cling exclusively to Saint-Saëns, Dvorak, and Elgar."[42] More important, to those who are interested in all film music, Dale presents a thoughtful answer to those "carping critics" who denigrate Korngold and other film composers. He particularly singles out Andre Previn, whose remarks on a "recent" TV show Dale thinks "were actuated by what the Germans call 'schadenfreude.' "[43]

Erich Wolfgang Korngold's concert compositions from his films are available on records. "Tomorrow," the symphonic tone poem from *The Constant Nymph*, is included in "The Sea Hawk, the Classic Film Scores of Erich Wolfgang Korngold," played by the National Philharmonic Orchestra, conducted by Charles Gerhardt, with Norma Procter, contralto, the Ambrosian Singers, and a women's chorus (RCA Record LSC-3330 STEREO). "The Escape Me Never Suite," including themes from the ballet "Primavera," is in the same record.

The Cello Concerto, heard in *Deception*, is included in "Elizabeth and Essex, the Classic Film Scores of Erich Wolfgang Korngold," played by the National Philharmonic Orchestra, conducted by Charles Gerhardt, with Francisco Gabarto, cellist (RCA Record ARL 1-0185 STEREO).

Prestigious film composer Franz Waxman was also given an opportunity to create serious music compositions, for *Humoresque* (1947). The works were adaptations, rather than originals, but they are still musically noteworthy: fantasias on *Carmen* and *Tristan und Isolde*, played by Isaac Stern (doubling for John Garfield) and symphony orchestra. Each work is performed at an important dramatic point in the story. The *Carmen Fantasia* is both better music and better suited to the film situation than the Wagner adaptation. In *Film Music Notes*, Louis Applebaum states: "The arguments that will undoubtedly be presented against a further rehashing and resetting of Bizet's already overplayed, almost hackneyed material, are suitably an-

Humoresque: **Oscar Levant and John Garfield.**

swered by Waxman's tasteful, colorful, even exciting treatment of this work."[44]

Applebaum is less enthusiastic about the musical merit of the *Tristan* piece, although he states that it is "an apt enough setting for the melodramatic romanticized suicide sequence."[45] Cinematically, however, the "Liebestod" is too apt, its inclusion so contrived that it does not function with any degree of subtlety. That audiences in 1947 accepted the suicide sequence, in which Joan Crawford walks into the surf as the radio reproduces Garfield's performance of the *Tristan Fantasia,* is more a tribute to the unique and stylized talent of Joan Crawford than to the powers-that-were who must have decided, in some mythical story conference, that the "Love-Death" music would be perfect for a "real" fictional filmed love-death.[46]

In 1968, director-lyricist Jacques Demy and Michel Legrand, himself the composer of romantic movie songs and background themes, presented a film, *The Young Girls of Rochefort,* intended as a follow-up to the highly successful

Rhapsody in Blue: **Robert Alda as George Gershwin; Oscar Levant as himself.**

film opera *Umbrellas of Cherbourg.* Although not acclaimed by either critics or audiences, the more recent picture is at once a charming musical and a spoof of musicals, particularly film biographies of musicians. In satire that is neither camp nor cruel, *The Young Girls* engagingly kids all the clichés of such films, and even features Gene Kelly in a parody of some of his well-known screen roles. Part of the movie's score is a piano concerto, supposedly written by Catherine Deneuve. Legrand's composition, in the style of Tchaikovsky, is appropriate to the overall romanticism of the film, and sounds very much like what one might expect the heroine-composer to have written. She plays the entire concerto (actually·performed by composer Legrand) at the end of the film. The composition has a great deal of lyrical charm and some sly humor, almost as if Legrand is poking a little fun not only at the romantic composers of the nineteenth century, but also at himself.

Although the "Theme du Concerto" has been published and can be heard on the sound-track album of the film, there is no recording or published sheet music of the entire concerto. The merits of both the *Young Girls of Rochefort* concerto and the film itself make them likely candidates for rediscovery. The score won an Academy Award nomination in 1969, but otherwise neither the film nor its music has really been recognized. In time, perhaps, both will be reevaluated by film and music critics.

Delicious (1931) has been written off by critics as a second-rate film; George Gershwin's Second Rhapsody is generally considered by music critics to be one of his lesser works. So why be excited about the fact that the rhapsody was an important piece of source music in *Delicious?* There are some important reasons.

First, the milieu of the Fox Studio in 1931 made it possible for George Gershwin to pursue his primary ambitions in serious composition. He wrote the rhapsody, substantially as it emerged in its final longer version, for the film, and was encouraged to complete the work by producer-executive Winfield Sheehan and studio executive William Fox. Second, the rhapsody *does* represent a development in Gershwin's compositional technique and, if not the widely acclaimed piece that *Rhapsody in Blue* was, is an interesting, highly underrated composition.

In an early scene in *Delicious*, Raul Roulien, playing a young composer, explains to Janet Gaynor the various motifs of the *Rhapsody in Rivets* he is writing.

He plays the slow theme (section 21 of the orchestra score) on the piano. Then he says, "The great towers, almost in the clouds," and plays the allegro, section 1. "Down below, in the long furrows, human seeds trying to grow to the light"; he plays section 2, as it will be heard for full orchestra. "And noise"—piano chords, section 3— "steel riveters, drumming your ear from every side"—six measures before section 8. "And this is the night motif"— the piano theme from section 5—"silencing the rivets." He continues to play as the camera cuts to another scene.

Later in the film, what was at the time of the picture's production the full-length version of the rhapsody is heard. (The film version is 7 minutes long; the published orchestral score runs 12.5 minutes.) At least two books about George Gershwin's life and music state that only one minute of the rhapsody is heard in *Delicious*.[47] Obviously the authors have not seen the film. Although the composition is performed by piano and full orchestra, what is unfortunate about the performance is that at times it must fight the battle of sound effects, which drown out some sections of the composition, and that the piano is barely audible at other times.

Marvin Maazel, who played the piano solo in the film recording, and who also appears in *Delicious*, has stated that when the music was being recorded, the piano was placed at the rear of the orchestra. He blames director David Butler for this arrangement. Butler, Maazel said, "feared the music would be distracting to the action."[48]

Hugo Friedhofer, who worked closely with Gershwin on the orchestration of the rhapsody, has told how the sequence in which the music is heard was put together.[49] Friedhofer consulted with Gershwin almost daily, and laid out the first orchestral sketch from the composer's two-line sketches. The piece was scored by the studio orchestra from Gershwin's final orchestration, which he sent to California after he had returned to New York. According to Friedhofer, some cuts were made in the film to accommodate the music, which was prescored, but some music cuts were also necessary.

Originally George Gershwin was to have returned to California for the music scoring, but did not do so. It has not been possible to determine who did the conducting for the film music, but it was probably Fox musical director Samuel Kaylin.

The sequence in which the full rhapsody is heard begins as Janet Gaynor, a fugitive from the immigration authorities, hides in the apartment of Raul Roulien. El Brendel, a friend, enters the scene and warns them that the authorities are coming up the stairs to seize Janet. She goes out a window to the fire escape, while Raul and his piano trio pretend to be rehearsing. They begin to play the rhapsody—but a special version of it. Hugo Friedhofer had to

Hugo Friedhofer, who adapted George Gershwin's Second Rhapsody for *Delicious*. (Photo by Irene Atkins).

write an introduction to the score that would make it possible for the music to begin as source music, and then become background scoring. The piano trio, which is photographed, plays a transcription of the slow theme, a violin and viola duet (section 24 in the printed score). As the camera reveals Janet Gaynor running down the fire escape and into the streets of New York, a chord signifies the segue into the actual orchestration of the rhapsody. She wanders through the streets, momentarily contemplating suicide on the bank of the East River, and finally gives

Delicious: left to right, **Marvin Maazel, who performed George Gershwin's Second Rhapsody on the sound track of the film; El Brendel; Manya Roberti.**

herself up at a police station. All the while, the Second rhapsody punctuates and underscores her confusion and helplessness as she walks through the city. That the rhapsody works well as accompaniment to the scenes is in a large part due to Friedhofer's smooth transition from source music to source scoring. (In the script of *Delicious,* the camera frequently cuts back to the trio playing the rhapsody, but these shots are not in the film.)

That Gershwin felt encouraged enough to continue working on the composition after his assignment on the film was finished, that he completed the work to his satisfaction, and that the early version of it remains on the Fox film sound track, are all historically important to the study of Gershwin and his music. About the writing of the rhapsody for the film, Gershwin has said: "In the picture, a composer comes to the United States, and I wanted to

Delicious: a nightclub performance. *Left to right,* Janet Gaynor, Marvin Maazel, Mischa Auer, Raul Roulien, Manya Roberti.

write music to express the composer's emotional reactions to New York. The work developed beyond the first conception, and so the title was changed from *Rhapsody in Rivets* to Second Rhapsody."[50]

Dr. Edward Kilenyi, Gershwin's theory teacher, has added his own recollections of the Second Rhapsody, in an unpublished monograph, *Gershwiniana,* which was written in 1963, given to Ira Gershwin, and placed in the Gershwin Archives. (A copy has also been given to the UCLA Music Library.) Dr. Kilenyi states (pp. 58–62):

> Now let me give here my own personal and musical account and experiences with George and his Second Rhapsody.
> At one of my visits to his home I found him in a happy

mood. He showed me the orchestral score of his latest
finished work, called then "Rhapsody in Rivets." On an
easily movable table were the large score-pages of the
orchestrations, also several thin pens, the kind used by
architects. So many lines had the orchestration required
that these score papers were printed to the special need
of the score. Almost at once he started to talk of the
finished work and searchingly, with a touch of anxiety,
he expressed some doubt of a possible weakness in the
form of the composition. "I wonder how Goetschius
would analyze it," he said. Thus he has shown his appreciation and respect for the author (who at that time was
still active in spite of his advanced age) of the textbook
we used. [NOTE: The text is *The Material Used in Musical
Composition*, by Percy Goetschius, published by G. Schirmer, New York, 1923.] I suggested that he should play
the whole composition for me on the piano. Also, that
during the playing he should explain to me what he was
doing thematically. This suggestion he accepted approv-
ingly and happily. I asked him also to stop after sections
of the form so that I should be able to make notes and
some sort of a chart in which he could see perspectively
the outline of the whole form of his entire composition.
He moved the table close to the piano. Then, while I
followed the score, he played it, and after every section
he explained his themes, his thematic developments, etc.
After the finish of this precious to remember demon-
stration, my first remark was that his main theme was, as
some of the other themes were, of rhythmic character
rather than singably melodious. He agreed. Then we
analyzed the form. We agreed with the form-fitting
terms.

Then, not thinking of my principle NOT to tell him to
make any changes to make them sound as if I or "somebody else would have composed it," I calmly observed:
"At the finishing climactic end the piano solo part has
nothing to play! You would just sit there doing nothing
while the audience might be even waiting for you to
continue to play! They might forget to applaud!" His
answer was, "But even if I should play, the full orchestra
would drown out the piano." "True enough," I said, and
went on elaborating on the idea. Not a teacher-made

exact suggestion of how the change could be made. He realized that my impression was worthwhile to consider. He actually asked me for exact musical details of what should be done to gain the desired and needed effect. I told him: "Before the final finishing bars the use of the main theme would be effective and would make the listener remember the main melodic theme of the whole composition." [NOTE: That is the form that is heard in *Delicious.*]

He became pleased. He sat down again at the piano and played a new finish according to the suggested idea. I surely loved what he played, and at once he put it down on paper.

It just happened that as soon as he did so, Bill Daly, for years his conductor and friend, came in. George enthusiastically told him, "Look, Bill, what changes Edward suggested for the finish of the Rhapsody." They sat down at the two pianos, side by side. Daly played the orchestral part, George the solo part—and both of them were pleased, indeed.

In our subsequent talking about the new work, he spoke of a choice of several possible titles, not one of them satisfactory to him. I remarked simply, "Why not simply call it Second Rhapsody?" They liked the idea at once and decided on it as the definite title. Our conversation drifted to the thrill we would have hearing the work performed. He said he would arrange some kind of a rehearsal and recording and he would let me know when, because he would like me to hear it. About a month later or so he phoned and invited me for a private recording at the National Broadcasting Company.

At my arrival in the studio he came to greet me. So did the NBC musical director, Erno Rapee. The rehearsal was conducted first by George. Then Bill Daly took it over with George playing the solo part.

A recording of that performance has been preserved. While visiting Ira Gershwin, Lawrence D. Stewart found "78s" of it in a closet where other records were stored. Ira Gershwin lent the records to NBC engineers, who made a copy. Mark 56 Records then received permission to copy a tape that had been made of those originals, and it has been released as part of the album "Gershwin by Gershwin," Mark 56 Records no. 641.

About the sound tracks that were made during the filming of *Delicious*, Dr. Kilenyi recalled:

In about 1951, in a lecture I was requested to give on the subject of film music in a large theater for the music departments of the schools of Greater Los Angeles, I had only a part of the original music track played because the complete track would have been too long for the occasion. Naturally it was listened to with intense interest. I suggested to the [Fox] studio music department that they should give a print of the full music track to the Library of Congress. I was anxious that the studio music department, of which I was a member for twenty-five years, should somehow be remembered in connection with the history of one of Gershwin's works. As far as I know now—1961—nothing has been done about this idea, and with everything that could have happened, perhaps all old music prints, positive and negative, might have been destroyed or lost.

The sound tracks of the rhapsody have never been found at the Twentieth Century–Fox Studios.

The Second Rhapsody contains moments of the best of George Gershwin. The premiere public performance took place at Symphony Hall in Boston on 29 February 1932, with the composer as piano soloist with the Boston Symphony Orchestra, conducted by Serge Koussevitsky. Since then, it has been performed infrequently. But at the University of Miami Gershwin Festival, held in October 1970, the Second Rhapsody was part of the opening-night program and received an enthusiastic audience response and highly favorable reviews. Doris Reno, in the *Miami Herald*, 28 October 1970, wrote, "The Rhapsody, which we like much better than 'Rhapsody in Blue,' engages the ear and nerves, and to some extent the imagination; it gives the pianist more scope than 'Blue' does."

In addition to the "Gershwin by Gershwin" recording,

the Second Rhapsody has been recorded several times, but many of the recordings are out of print. Those which are still available are by Leonard Pennario with Alfred Newman conducting the Hollywood Bowl Symphony Orchestra (Angel SP-8581); Jeffrey Siegel with Leonard Slatkin conducting the Saint Louis Symphony (Vox SVBX-5132); and Veri and Jamanis, two pianos (Connoisseur Society 2067).

Parts of the Second Rhapsody were used in the ballet *The New Yorkers,* with choreography by Leonide Massine and reorchestration by David Raksin, performed by the Ballets Russes de Monte Carlo.

Ethnic Source Music

Ethnomusicology, as defined by Jaap Kunst, is:

The study of *any* music, not only in terms of itself but also in relation to its cultural context. Currently the term has two broad applications: 1) the study of all music outside the European tradition in Europe and elsewhere, and 2) the study of all varieties of music found in one locale or region, i.e., all music being used by the people of a given area.[51]

In the cinematic context, particularly in the study of source music, ethnomusicology presents two important types for research: performed music in historical films, and similar music in those whose background is an exotic culture where, even in the present day, non-Western music prevails.

Certainly the outstanding composer of film music for historical films is Miklos Rozsa, whose scores cover the time span from *Quo Vadis* (1951) to *Plymouth Adventure* (1952). He has said, about his own work:

It is interesting to note what painstaking research is usually made to ascertain the year of publication of, let us say, "Yes, We Have No Bananas," if it is to be used in a picture about the Twenties, but no one seems to care much if the early Christians in the 1st century A.D. sing "Onward, Christian Solders" by Sir Arthur Sullivan, composed 1800 years later.[52]

Yet Rozsa seems to care a great deal about the source music in the films he has scored. In the same article about the music for *Quo Vadis,* he mentions that there were three distinct types of what he calls "on stage music" to be utilized. One was the music of the Romans, such as the songs of Nero. Rozsa used the *Skolion* or drinking song of the Graeco-Sicilian composer Seikilos for one of these.[53] Another type of music that was used was Greek, and a Greek hymn was used. For the third type, the music of the slaves, he used music of Babylonian, Syrian, Egyptian, and Persian origin.

Rozsa also devoted a great deal of study to the use of the instruments in source-music applications, relying on modern instruments to simulate the sounds of the prototypes of ancient Rome.[54] Studies of antique statues and vases gave clues to just what instruments should be used. The articles mentioned here give a good résumé of just how the scores of Rozsa's films were written.

In the scoring of films that may take place in the present or the recent past, but whose locales are places where non-Western music is predominant, a different set of problems presents itself to the composer. Bronislaw Kaper dealt with some of these problems in the scoring of *Lord Jim* (1965). *Lord Jim* is a heavy, brooding film, based on the novel that is generally considered to be one of Joseph Conrad's finest works. Kaper's thoughtful background score and the Indo-Chinese music that is used as source music form a blend of sound that helps to sustain the mood of other times and places. In some scenes, the "source" of the music is, perhaps deliberately, obscure. There *might* be a native group playing—out of camera range—or the music might be pure background. In all, the effect of the music is of "the mysterious East," and of a time when the locale of the novel and the film was less accessible than it is today.

Bronislaw Kaper, composer of *Lord Jim*, at home with his devoted cat. (Photo by Irene Atkins)

In an oral history, Mr. Kaper discussed some of the problems of recording the proper source music for *Lord Jim*.[55] His remarks give an insight into the workings of the Hollywood studio system in the 1960s. The following is an excerpt from the transcript.

BRONISLAW KAPER:
I used to work with Richard Brooks. We did *Brothers Karamazov*. One day he called me—this is so typical . . . and let's say it's Monday, and he said, "Can you be in Cambodia Friday, in Pnom Phenh?" Well, that's like saying, "Can you have lunch at the Bistro?" I said, "What's involved?" He said, "I'm doing *Lord Jim*. You've got to do it. It's a wonderful picture, Joseph Conrad." . . . When you work for a big studio, nothing is impossible. All the formalities that would otherwise take two or three weeks, they do in one day. Sometimes they give you a vaccination without your being around, even. They get somebody who gets you anyplace. You get a visa. You get a passport. It was maybe a little more than three days, maybe next week or something. But it was enough time for them to arrange everything, and for me to get the script.

That's how the madness started. Richard is an extremely talented man, and very strong in his convictions about what he's doing. . . .

Richard and I would sit and read the script, and then we discussed all the music, ahead of time, dramatically, not the notes. And that's why I like to work with him, because he really understood the meaning. It's got to have meaning.

Now, the picture was shot in Cambodia, but it could have been any of the countries there, in Laos, or any of them. Cambodia was chosen because of the Angkor Wat. I went there . . . to get the sound of native music. It didn't have to be exactly Cambodian . . . as long as it had the specific sound of a *gamelan* orchestra, which consists of certain instruments, of certain scales. Every one of those countries uses them differently. The sound is a little different. The scale is a little different—more or less brilliant; more or less dull.

. . . I went to Cambodia. We had a meeting there. It was preshooting. Richard was there, the cameraman, the soundman, and maybe the art director, and myself.

My purpose was to listen to Cambodian instruments and groups. I had a man there, a Cambodian, who knew music and who was a kind of adviser. He took me to different villages. We would drive three or four hours through the country, to get to a small village where there was a little singing group—old people, young people, no teeth, you know, but exotic. But what they performed was the dullest, absolutely impossible kind of music, which would die in the picture and drag the picture to death with it.

So we were terribly disappointed. And there was no variety of instruments. So the time I spent in Cambodia was completely fruitless. The only good thing was that I saw Cambodia and met the people. . . .

I left Cambodia terribly disappointed about my job. . . . The problem was that I could not use [the] Cambodian character of [the] *gamelan*, because it was dull, uninspired, limited, without any character. Our picture needed more life and more character and excitement. The problems were: how to get access to this music, to learn some kind of *gamelan* music; how to learn to write it, because it's a different scale, with different notation; where to get the instruments, if we could find out what instruments we need; and where to get the people who can play these instruments. Now these were enough problems for me not to sleep. I just didn't know what to do. I discussed it with Richard. Fantasies entered our minds, like somebody said, "There are two French students who study this kind of *gamelan* music, and they live in Paris, and one of them had one of these instruments built in Paris." Fantasies. Nightmares.

There then was a question about contacting the Indo-Chinese Embassy in Amsterdam. *They* were supposed to have some kind of a collection. Then there was a question that in London maybe the museum has some kinds of instruments, and we could get access. We talked and we walked, and I was sweating, and I didn't know what to do, until one day I talked to a man who used to be my agent, Abe Meyer, who was with MCA. I talked to him, because we talked all the time about it. He said, "Did you call Mantle Hood at UCLA? The ethnomusicology department—he's the head of it. He can help you."

I phoned Mantle Hood, and introduced myself. He said, "I know you very well. We met before." He was a very serious composer and musician. He used to study with Ernst Toch. I made an appointment with him. I went to UCLA, and he took me downstairs in the music building. He said, "I will take you now to the *gamelan* room." When I heard this, already I felt better. He took me, took the key, and opened the door. . . . There was a room with all the *gamelan* instruments you want—Bali, Java, Thailand, every one of them. At a certain point— they were on the floor—I was trying to step over one instrument, and he said, excitedly, "A-a, a-a! This is Java. You're not supposed to step over this." Any other instruments, yes, but Java, you're not allowed to step over. Of course I didn't know it. I was naive. Now I know. I would never step over a Javanese instrument.

Anyway, he had all the *gamelan* instruments of all the different Indo-Chinese nations. He had a steady *gamelan* orchestra, which was composed of UCLA students and some outsiders. He had coaches, two women associates of his. They had a rehearsal every week. Now, I had to decide which *gamelan* I was going to use, which sound. The winner was Bali. . . . The picture does not mean Cambodia. And the music of Bali was really very exciting.

He showed me the recordings they made, and I was listening and listening. And then I started the Indo-Chinese-ation of Bronislaw Kaper. I got from him all the charts about the instruments. I took orchestration lessons, like I would do it in a Western country in a conservatory. I listened to every instrument. I was taught the range of it; what's easy, what's difficult; how you play them, how they sound together. I studied the score. I studied how they write it, because they have a completely different method. They don't have the names like we have, *C, C* sharp. They have numbers. Everything is different. The tuning is different. It's tuned in quarter-tones. That's why it sounds so strange. The sounds merge, and work into each other. They hear one player playing what we would call *C* sharp, and the other plays *D* flat, and there's a difference.

The difference in *gamelan* music in different countries is in the substance of the music, first of all. Sometimes the instruments overlap, and you can find them in different countries—except when you go to a country like Japan. *Gagaku*. I learned this, too.

. . . I was coming to rehearsals. I was listening, studying orchestration, and one day came the moment of truth. I had to write something. So I wrote two pieces, one slow, one fast. I wrote two scores and gave them to Mantle Hood, to be rehearsed the next day.

Being chicken, I didn't go to the rehearsal. I just wanted to leave them alone to practice, because the practicing is also fantastic, the way they rehearse. The fast passages in the music are not played by one instrument. They are played by two, and one of them plays the downbeat, and the other one plays the second, fourth, and sixth note. So one plays [CLAPS HANDS AND SINGS IN STRICT RHYTHM] bahm, bahm, bahm, bahm. The other does [CLAPS ON BEAT AND SINGS OFF THE BEAT] da, da, da, da. You would call it really syncopation, but it's not. It's just that together you get a martellato effect. And how this other instrument plays against the beat, I don't know. It's fantastic. But they do.

I wrote those two pieces. I called Mantle and I said, "How did it go?" He said, "Well, the slow piece, like a charm. The fast piece was unplayable." I said, "What happened?" He said, "Well, in two instruments you thought they are being played with two hands, but they are played with one hand." Take a xylophone: if you do two hands you play a fast passage. If you play with one hand, your wrist cannot play that fast. So I rewrote it later, and it was playable. But for the moment, I thought there was tragedy. Anyway, that's how I learned this whole thing.

While I was there, at the same time, being a gourmet, I learned to write for Japanese *gagaku*, because it was fascinating. As a matter of fact, at the end of *Lord Jim*, I smuggled in a little piece which had a little of the *gagaku* character, regardless of geography, and all this. After he dies, after his funeral, I used this high oboe that they have, and the drums. It's an unbelievable effect.

This was my acquaintance with the music, but you see it was all by accident. We recorded a lot of music, *almost* wild. Some of the music we recorded to the picture. Some of it was just wild recording. And then we played with it. We took the tracks, and spaced them, wherever we could. Now the actual scoring of the movie was in London. I spent a few months there. Muir Mathieson, who is a terrific guy in musicianship, in temperament, was the conductor. And I had a fabulous time with him.

We took the tracks of the *gamelan* music, which had been recorded at UCLA, to London. I went with a whole entourage: Robert Franklyn, the orchestrator— unfortunately he's dead now—and his wife, and the most important one, Peter Zinner, the music cutter. You cannot do a great movie, great in the sense of bigness and complications and problems, without having a first- rate music cutter, especially when you deal not only with regular scoring, but with cutting to wild tracks. Peter Zinner is an excellent musician and a wonderful movie man. He understands movies and is bright and intelli- gent. I took him with me. . . .

The recordings were a job. The English orchestra was fantastic. They had people there who were absolutely masters, in every respect. . . .

. . . Peter Zinner did a fantastic job. . . . He is a fabu- lous man and easy to be with, and understands things.

There is a lot of music in the picture. Comparatively, there is not that much ethnic music. Unfortunately, they dubbed the picture in England, and I was already here, because it was much later. Not every part of the picture was dubbed the way I would have liked to have it. But, then, if you're not there, there is nothing you can do. I'm sure that if I were there, I would discuss things with Richard. He was very bright.

Lord Jim was a great experience for me. I saw elements put together which were terribly difficult. I saw, really, magic come out of this mixing of native music with the Western score.

Mr. Kaper mentioned, concerning both the trip to Cambodia and the one to London, the great numbers of people in the studio entourages and the lavishness of the hotel accommodations. "You don't see those things any more," he said.[56] The whole idea of a studio so precipitously sending the composer to Cambodia (or anyplace else) to find suitable music is probably a thing of the past, too.

Dr. Mantle Hood, formerly Professor of Music and Director of the Institute of Ethnomusicology at UCLA, and now a member of the faculty of the University of Indiana, reviewed Mr. Kaper's transcript and offered to add his own comments on it as well as his recollections of the recording of the music for *Lord Jim*. These comments are reproduced here, with Dr. Hood's permission.[57]

DR. MANTLE HOOD:

I thought this might be the fastest way to make a few comments about *Lord Jim* and my participation in it. I read what you typed out of the interview with Bronislaw Kaper, and to the best of memory, his recall seems excellent. That's very much the working relationship we had. I might elaborate just a little bit.

I remember the first evening, when Kaper brought Richard Brooks and his lovely wife, Jean Simmons, down to our large holdings in the basement of the music building, to hear some of this music. The students were all thrilled, of course, to be able to meet Jean Simmons, although I don't believe many of them had heard of Richard Brooks. We played quite a large variety of different kinds of music from Southeast Asia. And ultimately, in four nights of recording at Columbia Pictures, we recorded many different kinds—I'm not sure in actual time—I think possibly a total of two hours of sound. The amount actually used in the film I've never really totaled up. It was far less than that. So somewhere somebody has a lot in reserve, and it probably will be continued to be used in future motion pictures, if it has the right setting.

There are one or two things that might amuse you. In the course of four nights of recording, my wife was a participant in the large Balinese *gamelan* orchestra. And the union was there, very much in evidence. But I think there were not more than two or three of our performers who were union members, but the union required that a representative be there, and the kids were all paid union wages. After the motion picture came out and there was a recording of the music, they also collected residuals for several years. I think we had about forty or fifty performers involved. At any rate, back to my little story about the union representative—my wife not only was a participant in the *gamelan,* but she was about eight months and twenty-eight days pregnant. And the union representative every night was afraid she was going to have to run and get boiling water. The fact is we finished recording, I think, on the fourth night, and, believe it or not, on the fifth night my wife gave birth. So that was close timing.

One other thing I recall: initially we had a little problem with the actual technicalities of recording this kind of music, because the union people responsible for this at Columbia Pictures, of course, had never recorded anything except the standard Western orchestra. And a lot of struck gongs and bronze slabs and wooden keys and such things do require a slightly different technique. So the first evening, one of the principal soundmen, who'd been with MGM for thirty years, was sitting in on this with Kaper. He was in charge. As yet we hadn't recorded a note. I decided we'd start with a little five-piece ensemble from Java, which plays a little modal prelude. And I'll never forget—we sat there for at least—it seemed an hour; it was probably twenty minutes—waiting for the microphone men, the special category in the union, to place the microphones properly so that we could hear this sound in the control booth. And finally Kaper was just wringing his hands. He said, "My God! It doesn't sound like this when you're actually present. It's no good. What are we going to do?"

"Well," I said, "if the union won't throw me in jail, maybe I can go down and make a suggestion or two."

He said, "My God, do!" So I did. I went down to the floor, down below the control booth, where the musicians were performing. I wasn't allowed to touch a mike, by the union. I couldn't put my hand on one. But I did place my hand in midair at the various positions that we had. We had placed, I think, four or five microphones. I had been recording this kind of music in the field, that is, in Java and Southeast Asia, for about twenty years, so I knew a little about it. Then we did a first trial, after the replacement of mikes. And from the control booth, over the PA system, one wonderful word from Broni: "Beautiful." And from then on, I was in charge of placing mikes, but only with my hand in midair. I wasn't allowed to touch them.

When we were finished, we came back then to hear the playbacks, in the big studio they have there. I've forgotten how many channels they used; at least sixteen; it might have been twenty-four or thirty-two. I don't really remember. It was *enormous*. And as we walked in, this man from MGM told me, when we were walking together, "Dr. Hood, I heard this, this morning, and as far as I'm concerned, they can burn down the goddamned studio. They'll never get anything close to this again." And I must say, when I heard it played back, I couldn't believe my ears. It was a fantastic recording.

I was disappointed, however, when the film actually came out, because they dubbed down, they cut down the sound of the big Balinese *gamelan* and some of the others. And I have to conclude that it was because by contrast the Western symphony indeed seemed very pale. Even though, if I remember correctly, I think the Balinese *gamelan* was in some of the title music, they were anxious, I guess, that this foreign idiom not supersede and in any sense detract from the magnificence of the symphony orchestra.

Well, those are just a few little asides. I had a lot of fun working on this show with Kaper, and we worked together easily, in the following way:

He wrote a melody that was used for the large Balinese *gamelan*. That was one that caused problems. His orchestrator just threw up his hands the first or second night, I think, of hearing this stuff. He didn't know what to do with it, obviously. So Kaper wrote a melody for this Balinese *gamelan*, and then I sort of became *de facto* his orchestrator, in a sense—that is, I at least was able to put that melody in the idiom of the various instruments. There are thirty or more in the Balinese *gamelan*. And I assisted in this way: I remember at one point, he'd written something, and we were discussing it over the telephone. I said, "Broni, that's just too fast. They can't play that fast, because they're wielding hammers."

Broni said, "Now, wait a minute. Listen to this." So he held the telephone near the piano keys. And, of course, he ripped it off with his fingers. When he came back on, I said, "Look, you're just moving ten fingers, but these people are moving their whole arm. They have to hit once each time with an arm movement. They're fast, very fast; they're not *that* fast." Well, anyhow, we finally got it together and, in order to satisfy the kind of image he had, we played at an unbelievable speed. I think I can say with confidence that it was faster even than is required of traditional Balinese *gamelan*. And that's unbelievably fast.

I admired Mr. Kaper very much for his ability to very quickly perceive and penetrate foreign idioms of expression. I won't say that he emerged a replete composer within them. That would be unfair to him and to the traditions. But he did a remarkably fine job in our Japanese and *gagaku* ensemble, which is the old court orchestra of the imperial household. It goes back to the eighth century in a continuous tradition. We handed him a score. In that particular music, there have been some transcriptions in Western notation. And he studied that, and on the strength of it, he wrote another piece that was acceptably within the tradition. I'm not sure they would incorporate it into the palace repertory, but he really did an excellent job.

One last point that might interest you. I think he mentioned that Richard Brooks was very nervous about cutting the film; that is, he didn't want people watching over his shoulder. I gather he had a bad experience on an early film. I think it might have been *Cat on a Hot Tin Roof.* He had some new techniques, and somebody saw the rushes and stole them and got a film out before he did. So the result was I could really have been of much more help had I been allowed to see the film and give some advice and suggestions in the actual putting of music to scene. But at first he said that would be fine, as long as Broni and I saw it in short segments unrelated. But finally he even cancelled that. So I wasn't allowed to work in that way—with the result that there were a few things that I would have objected to if I'd had any right to object. I'm not sure they would have listened.

But the Japanese and *gagaku* music was used, in fact, to accompany what was visually something that looked close to a Balinese cremation ceremony. Now, Balinese are Hindu, and that would not work at all, of course, to have Japanese court music behind a Balinese cremation. But in addition, as I recall, the priest was wearing saffron robes, so it had a Buddhist look. Well, by a stretch of the imagination, *gagaku* ensembles do play in Buddhist temples. So that might have been different, but at least in terms of motion picture music and mood setting, it was the kind of thing that Kaper thought appropriate in that last scene. And to the extent that I can detach myself from all I know about that tradition and just try to listen to it as proper music for the mood, I would have to admit it did work pretty well.

Conclusion

The study of source music as represented in films of the last fifty years makes the researcher aware of one overwhelming fact: the plethora of source-music usage in fictional films, of thousands upon thousands of sequences involving source music. That fact has two implications: first, that no matter which films have been discussed in this book there must have been some whose omission will be regretted or even resented. Second, and more important, the overabundance of source-music examples is evidence that the device has sometimes been overworked, and at times misused.

Source music works best when it evolves naturally from the narrative, and not so well when it is an excuse for the inclusion of potential "sound-track hits" or when it tells the audience "where the music is coming from." A small, but significant, renaissance of symphonic background scoring in recent films gives a promise that a little gold may still glitter in the ages to come of film music. Such a development, one that frees the filmmaker from self-consciousness about background music, can help improve the climate for dramatically and musically valid and creative source music, too. The source-music sequence represents a challenge, a quest for something innovative in a traditional form.

To the filmmaker, source music can be an exciting means of communication. It can, at the same time, afford a medium for new musical compositions—popular songs or concert works. But first the source music must work within the film, as part of a total creative effort.

Notes

1. Robert Emmett Dolan, *Music in Modern Media* (New York: G. Schirmer, 1967), p. 180. © copyright, 1967, by G. Schirmer, Inc. Used by permission.

2. Tony Thomas, *Music for the Movies* (South Brunswick and New York: A. S. Barnes and Co., 1973), p. 15.

3. Robert U. Nelson, "Film Music: Color or Line?," *Hollywood Quarterly* 2 (October 1946): 57.

4. "As Times Goes By" was written by Herman Hupfeld for the musical show *Everybody's Welcome* in 1931.

5. *The Jazz Singer,* although hailed as the first talkie—even being thus celebrated by a commemorative U.S. postage stamp—was preceded by other films in which there was talking and singing.

6. For some reason, "needle drops"—scenes depicting someone playing a record—are prevalent in killing scenes, particularly those at the hands of gangsters. A memorable murder scene occurs in *Al Capone* (1958), when Big Jim Colisimo, an Italian gang leader, is killed as he listens to a Caruso record. Jay Gatsby (in *The Great Gatsby* [1974]) is shot just after he starts the phonograph playing "When You and I Were Seventeen" (words: Gus Kahn; music: Charles Rosoff).

7. Personal interview with Bryan Foy, 29 August 1973.

8. Charles Higham and Joel Greenberg, *The Celluloid Muse* (New York: Henry Regnery C., 1969), p. 148.

9. Roger Manvell and John Huntley, *The Technique of Film Music* (New York: Hastings House, 1957, rev. 1967), p. 49. Published by Focal Press, Inc., 10 East 40 Street, New York, New York 10016. Used by permission.

10. The music award was won by Louis Silvers for *One Night of Love.*

11. Thomas, p. 113.

12. Peter Bogdanovich, *John Ford* (Berkeley: University of California Press, 1968), p. 99.

13. J. A. Place, *The Western Films of John Ford* (Secaucus, N.J.: Citadel Press, 1974), p. 82.

14. Elmer Bernstein, "What Ever Happened to Great Movie Music?," *High Fidelity,* July 1972, p. 55. David Raksin, in "Whatever Became of Movie Music?," *Film Music Notebook,* Fall 1974, gives another view.

15. This criticism is based, of course, on the fact that Bing Crosby was very much alive at the time of the film's release.

16. "I Only Have Eyes for You," sung by the Flamingos in *American Graffiti,* would have been appropriate in *Paper Moon.* It was written in 1934 by Harry Warren and Al Dubin and was first heard in the Dick Powell–Joan Blondell musical film *Dames.*

17. Richard Combs, "American Graffiti," *Monthly Film Bulletin*, February 1974, p. 23.

18. The scoring of *The Exorcist* and the firing of Lalo Schifrin are discussed in *Dialogue on Film*, vol. 3, no. 4 (1974), and Elmer Bernstein, "The Annotated Friedkin," *Film Music Notebook*, Winter 1974–75.

19. David Raksin considers the tango, in the gambling-boat sequence of the film, the best piece of source music in *What's the Matter with Helen?*

20. Personal interview with John Green, June 1972.

21. Arthur Knight, liner notes, *They Shoot Horses, Don't They?*, ABC Records ABCS-OC-10-Stereo.

22. In a personal interview on 5 March 1974 Jack Clayton was told about John Green's two-year capacity as producer and musical director, and was asked why he hadn't had a musical director on the set during the shooting of *Gatsby*. "I suppose," he said, with a slight smile, "it's because I'm a complete megalomaniac." In the same interview, though, Clayton mentioned how much he had liked the job Riddle had done.

23. Personal interview with Nelson Riddle, 15 February 1974.

24. F. Scott Fitzgerald, *The Great Gatsby* (New York: Charles Scribner's Sons, 1925), p. 39.

25. Oscar Levant, *A Smattering of Ignorance* (New York: Doubleday, Doran and Co., 1939), p. 114.

26. Levant, p. 117.

27. Ibid., p. 118.

28. Ibid.

29. Levant, p. 119. (The plural *producers* refers to John Stone and executive producer Sol Wurtzel.)

30. Ibid., p. 118.

31. Ibid.

32. Pauline Kael, *The Citizen Kane Book* (Boston: Atlantic–Little, Brown, 1971), p. 67.

33. Ibid., p. 67.

34. Christopher Palmer, liner notes, *Citizen Kane* by Bernard Herrmann, RCA/ARL 1-0707. Used by permission.

35. Charles Higham, *The Films of Orson Welles* (Berkeley: University of California Press, 1970).

36. Donald Jay Grout, *A Short History of Opera* (New York: Columbia University Press, 1965), pp. 323, 458, 523.

37. The film has not been viewed by the author, so no attempt has been made to describe the function of the composition within the film.

38. Manvell and Huntley, p. 65.

39. Hugo Friedhofer, Ray Heindorf, and Bernhard Kaun have all been given orchestration credit on *Four Daughters*.

40. George Korngold, liner notes, *The Sea Hawk*, RCA/LSC-3330.

41. Charles Higham and Joel Greenberg, *Hollywood in the Forties* (New York: A. S. Barnes and Co., 1968), p. 164.

42. S. S. Dale, "Contemporary Cello Concerti XLIII. Korngold and Penderecki," *The Strad,* August 1976, p. 281.

43. Dale, pp. 277–89.

44. Louis Applebaum, "Waxman and Humoresque," *Film Music Notes,* December–January 1946–47, p. 5.

45. Ibid., p. 6.

46. In 1935, motion picture actor John Bowers committed suicide by walking into the ocean, after he had started his phonograph playing "Red Sails in the Sunset." This actuality is the basis of the suicides in the 1937 and 1954 versions of *A Star Is Born;* in the 1954 film, James Mason dies as Judy Garland sings one of the movie's songs. The contrast of popular song and love-death, or even Bowers's sick sort of humor, makes the songs more appropriate to the scenes than Wagner.

47. David Ewen, *A Journey to Greatness* (New York: Henry Holt and Co., 1956), p. 211; and Robert Kimball and Alfred Simon, *The Gershwins* (New York: Atheneum, 1973), p. 132.

48. Personal interview with Marvin Maazel, 18 December 1977.

49. *Oral History with Hugo Friedhofer,* interviewed by Irene Kahn Atkins (Copyright, The American Film Institute, 1974), pp. 84–85. Material also taken from other personal interviews with Mr. Friedhofer.

50. "Gershwin Returns from Hollywood," *Watertown Daily Times,* 19 January 1932.

51. Mantle Hood, "Ethnomusicology," *Harvard Dictionary of Music,* 1969 edition, p. 298.

52. Miklos Rozsa, "Quo Vadis," *Film/TV Music,* November–December 1951, pages unnumbered.

53. Reproduced in *Wellsprings of Music* by Curt Sachs (New York: McGraw-Hill Book Company, 1965), p. 58.

54. Christopher Palmer, "Miklos Rozsa," *Performing Right,* May 1971, pp. 11–15.

55. *Oral History with Bronislaw Kaper,* interviewed by Irene Kahn Atkins, undertaken by the Film History Program of the American Film Institute, funded from a grant from the Louis B. Mayer Foundation (Copyright, The American Film Insitute, 1975), pp. 355–69. Excerpt reprinted with permission of the AFI.

56. *Oral History with Bronislaw Kaper,* p. 367.

57. Transcribed from a cassette sent to the author, August 1977.

References

Applebaum, Louis. "Waxman and Humoresque." *Film Music Notes,* December–January 1946–47.

Baxter, John. *The Cinema of John Ford.* London: Tantivy Press, 1971.

Bernstein, Elmer. "What Ever Happened to Great Movie Music?" *High Fidelity,* July 1972, pp. 55–58.

Bogdanovich, Peter. *John Ford.* Berkeley: University of California Press, 1968.

———. "The Kane Mutiny." *Esquire,* October 1972, pp. 99–105 +.

Dale, S. S. "Contemporary Cello Concerti: Korngold and Penderecki." *The Strad* 87, no. 1036 (August 1976): 277–89.

Dolan, Robert Emmett. *Music in Modern Media.* New York: G. Schirmer, 1967.

Ewen, David. *All the Years of American Popular Music.* Englewood Cliffs, N.J.: Prentice-Hall, 1977.

Ferguson, Stanley. "Gone with the Sound Track: Pit Orchestras." *New Republic,* 30 March 1942, pp. 426–27.

Geduld, Harry. *The Birth of the Talkies.* Bloomington: Indiana University Press, 1975.

Grout, Donald Jay. *A Short History of Opera.* New York: Columbia University Press, 1965.

Hagen, Earle. *Scoring for Films.* New York: E.D.J. Music; sole selling agent, Criterion Music Corp., 1971.

Higham, Charles. *The Films of Orson Welles.* Berkeley: University of California Press, 1970.

Higham, Charles and Joel Greenberg. *The Celluloid Muse.* New York: Henry Regnery Co., 1969.

———. *Hollywood in the Forties.* New York: Paperback Library, 1970.

125

Hood, Dr. Mantle. "Bali," "Ethnomusicology," and "Java," in *Harvard Dictionary of Music*, edited by Willi Appel. Cambridge, Mass.: Belknap Press, Harvard University Press, 1969.

"It's on the Sound Track." *Overture*, November 1964, p. 12.

Jablonski, Edward, and Milton Caine. "Gershwin's Movie Music." *Films in Review*, October 1951, pp. 23–28.

Jablonski, Edward, and Lawrence D. Stewart. *The Gershwin Years*. Garden City, N.Y.: Doubleday and Co., 1958.

Johnson, William. "Face the Music." *Film Quarterly*, Summer 1969, pp. 3–19.

Kael, Pauline. *The Citizen Kane Book*. New York: Atlantic–Little, Brown, 1971.

Keller, Hans. "Gershwin's Genius." *Musical Times*, November 1962, pp. 763–71.

Kimball, Robert, and Alfred Simon. *The Gershwins*. New York: Atheneum, 1973.

Knight, Arthur. "All Singing! All Talking! All Laughing! 1929, the Year of the Great Transition." *Theatre Arts Magazine*, September 1949, pp. 33–40.

Levant, Oscar. *A Smattering of Ignorance*. New York: Doubleday, Doran and Co., 1940.

London, Kurt. *Film Music*. London: Faber and Faber, 1936. Reprint. New York: Arno Press, 1970.

Malm, William P. *Music Cultures of the Pacific, the Near East, and Asia*. Englewood Cliffs, N.J.: Prentice-Hall, 1967.

Manvell, Roger, and John Huntley. *The Technique of Film Music*. London: Focal Press, 1957. Revised edition. 1967. Enlarged ed., New York: Hastings House, 1975.

Marema, Thomas. "The Sound of Movie Music." *New York Times Magazine*, 28 March 1976, pp. 40–48.

McCarty, Clifford. *Film Composers in America*. Glendale, Calif.: By the author, 1953. Reprint. New York: Da Capo Press, 1972.

McConnell, Stanlie. "Teaching Possibilities in Current Films: 'Deception.'" *Film Music Notes*, November 1946, p. 7.

Miller, Frank. "Analysis of the Korngold Cello Concerto." *Film Music Notes*, March 1964, pp. 20–24.

Milne, Tom. *Mamoulian*. Bloomington: Indiana University Press, 1970.

Nelson, Robert U. "Film Music: Color or Line?" *Hollywood Quarterly* 2 (October 1946): 57–65.

Palmer, Christopher. "Miklos Rozsa." *Performing Right,* May 1971, pp. 11–15.

Place, J. A. *The Western Films of John Ford.* Secaucus, N.J.: Citadel Press, 1974.

Raksin, David. "Whatever Became of Movie Music?" *Film Music Notebook* 1 (Fall 1974): 22–26.

"Richard Addinsell: British Film Music Composer." *Film Music Notes,* May 1946, pp. 33–34.

Sachs, Curt. *The Wellsprings of Music.* Edited by Jaap Kunst. New York: McGraw-Hill Book Co., 1965.

Schwartz, Charles. *Gershwin: His Life and Music.* Indianapolis and New York: Bobbs-Merrill Co., 1973.

Strunk, Oliver, ed. *Source Readings in Music History.* Vol. 1, *Antiquity and the Middle Ages.* New York: W. W. Norton and Co., 1965.

Thomas, Tony, *Music for the Movies.* South Brunswick and New York: A. S. Barnes and Co., 1973.

Winter, Marion H. "Function of Music in the Sound Film." *Musical Quarterly,* April 1941.

Zolotow, Maurice. *Billy Wilder in Hollywood.* New York: G. P. Putnam's Sons, 1977.

MORE THAN MEETS THE EYE

A Bibliography of Music and Sound in Motion Pictures

Bibliographies and Catalogs

ASCAP: 30 Years of Motion Picture Music. New York: The American Society of Authors, Composers, and Publishers, 1966.
    Writer and other film credits are listed chronologically, according to song titles.
"Composers on Film Music: A Bibliography." *Film,* Winter 1940.
    Brief; most references have been cited elsewhere.
Ellis, Jack C., and Charles Derry and Sharon Kern, with research assistance from Stephen E. Bowles. *The Film Book Bibliography.* Metuchen, N.J.: Scarecrow Press, 1979.
    An extensive bibliography, with several relevant sections, each of which is arranged chronologically. "Music," section 8, pp. 85–87, and a longer section, "Collective Biography, Analysis, and Interviews," pp. 349–69, contain annotations of many film-music resources.
Leonard, Harold. L., ed. *The Film Index, A Bibliography.* Vol. 1, *The Film as Art.* New York: The Museum of Modern Art and the H. W. Wilson Co., 1941. Reprint. New York: Arno Press, 1970.
    Listings of books and magazine articles about music of both the silent and sound eras, pp. 202–11. Also of musical interest are sections on sound, pp. 231–45, early sound effects and recording devices, pp. 245–49, and musical films, 468–72.
Leyda, Jay. "Film Literature, 1945." *Hollywood Quarterly,* Supplement to vol. 1, 1946. "Part 1, Film Techniques: Music," p. 4.
    A brief list, but of interest for some articles not listed elsewhere.

Lichtenwager, William and Carolyn. Compiled by Wayne D. Shirley. *Modern Music: An Analytic Index.* New York: Ames Press, 1976.

Well indexed and annotated, with many sections on film music, this guide to the magazine of avant-garde music of the 1920s, 1930s, and 1940s, published by the League of Composers, offers much worthwhile material.

MacCann, Richard Dyer, and Edward S. Perry. *The New Film Index: A Bibliography of Magazine Articles in English, 1930–1970.* New York: E. P. Dutton and Co., 1975.

A chronological subject index of film and general-interest magazines. Sections on music and sound. The introductory explanation of how the bibliography was compiled is helpful. A good companion to *The Film Index.*

Marks, Martin. "Film Music: The Material, Literature, and Present State of Research." *Music Library Association Notes,* December 1979.

A scholarly evaluation of just about everything written about film music serves as a preface to the bibliography, which is, as the author states, "selective." It is fully annotated, with sections listing books, periodicals, pamphlets, and dissertations.

Mehr, Linda Harris, ed. *Motion Pictures, Television, and Radio: A Union Catalogue of Manuscript and Special Collections in the Western United States.* Boston: G. K. Hall, 1977.

An important book, especially valuable to those interested in film music for its listings of film scores and papers of many film composers.

Nelson, Robert Q., and Walter Rubsamen. "Literature on Music in Film and Radio." *Hollywood Quarterly,* Supplement to vol. 1, 1946, pp. 40–42.

Excellent; very complete for books and magazine articles published up to the time of publication.

Parker, David, and Esther Siegel. *Guide to Dance in Film.* New York: Gale Research, 1978.

An index, including notes on many American musical films, with names of directors, dance directors, songwriters, and dancers. Useful for screen credit information.

Rehrauer, George. *Cinema Booklist.* Metuchen, N.J.: Scarecrow Press, 1972. Supplement 1, 1974; Supplement 2, 1977.

A valuable bibliography of books on film, with cross-indexing of various aspects of film music.

Rubsamen, Walter. "Literature on Music in Film and Radio: Addenda (1943–1948)." *Hollywood Quarterly* 3 no. 4 (Summer 1948): 403–7.
   Good supplement to the Nelson-Rubsamen listings; many references not cited elsewhere.

Sharples, Win. "A Selected and Annotated Bibliography of Books and Articles on Music in the Cinema." *Cinema Journal* 17, no. 2 (Spring 1978): 36–67.
   Very complete listings, plus listings of music clubs, record societies, and films about motion picture music.

Zuckerman, John W. "A Selected Bibliography on Music for Motion Pictures." *Hollywood Quarterly* 5 no. 2 (Winter 1950): 195–99.
   Not a great number of titles, but the list includes some not cited elsewhere.

Books on Film Music

Bazelon, Irwin. *Knowing the Score.* New York: Van Nostrand Reinhold, 1975.
   Bazelon is the Angry Young Man of film-music criticism, a kind of latter-day Eisler. His abrasiveness is distractive and detracts from his arguments, which are not exceptionally valid. The interview section is marred, also, by the opinionated, slanted questions.

Berg, Charles Merrell. *An Investigation of the Motives for and Realization of Music to Accompany the American Silent Film, 1896–1927.* New York: Arno Press, 1976.
   A study of how and why music was used during the silent era. A few of the many conclusions are based on conjecture, but generally the findings reflect extensive, in-depth research into book, periodical, and other resources of the period.

Colpi, Henri. *Defense et illustration de la musique dans le film.* Ain, France: Société d'Edition de Recherches et de Documentation Cinématographique, 1963.
   A limited reading knowledge of French will suffice for reading this thoughtful critical discussion of music in many films, both European and American. "La musico-filmographie" is quite extensive. Many photographs, and interesting facsimiles of scores and composers' sketches.

Eisler, Hanns. *Composing for the Films.* New York: Oxford University Press, 1947.
   This book is considered a "classic." It is perhaps characteris-

tic of the volume, which is actually a diatribe against Hollywood and "the culture industry" rather than a book about film music, that Eisler hasn't a word of praise for any film score except a few of his own. Many statements lack cogency, mainly because Eisler's deprecating view of films and their "illiterate" audience is anachronistic. Denunciations of Prokofiev's score for *Alexander Nevsky* and Eisenstein's analysis of it conclude the text.

Evans, Mark. *Soundtrack: The Music of the Movies.* New York: Hopkinson and Blake, 1975. Paperback reprint. New York: Da Capo Press, 1979.

This book's strength is that Mr. Evans has obviously met some of the key people who created film music; its weakness is that he hasn't met others. There are names and anecdotes that would appeal to the general reader who is interested in film music, but the book is not profound enough to attract serious technicians or scholars.

Faulkner, Robert. *Hollywood Studio Musicians: Their Work and Careers in the Recording Industry.* Chicago: Aldine Atherton, 1971.

A sociologist's view of the working musicians of Hollywood and their relationships to composers and musical directors. Perhaps too selective in its narrow base of interviewees, but most interesting.

Films for Music Education and Opera Films. Edited by International Music Centre, Vienna. Paris: UNESCO, 1964.

Listings and descriptions, intended mainly for educators seeking classroom material.

Films on Traditional Music and Dance. International Folk Music Council. Edited by Peter Kennedy. Paris: UNESCO, 1970.

"Traditional music" in the title means "folk music" to most readers. Listings of films by country, with credits and other pertinent information.

Hagen, Earle. *Scoring for Films.* New York: E.D.J. Music; sole selling agent, Criterion Music Corp., 1971.

Hagen's book presents for the trained musician a verbal and graphic orientation to the technique of writing music for theatrical films and filmed television. The first half of the book deals with technical details. The second is based on a symposium attended by Hagen and several other movie composers, and considers their work and philosophies. A practical, thorough work.

Huntley, John. *British Film Music.* London: Skelton Robinson, 1947. Reprint. New York: Arno Press, 1972.

A discussion of film music in general adds dimension to the later examination of music in British movies. Appendixes give data on composers and studio orchestras.

Knudson, Carroll. *Project Tempo.* Los Angeles: By the author, 1965.

A series of conversion tables to be used when scoring films with click tracks. Valuable to a composer or conductor using this technique.

Levy, Louis. *Music for the Movies.* London: Samson Low, Marston and Co., 1948.

Personalized anecdotal narrative of Levy's own work in film musicals and scoring of dramatic films, with a minimum of technical and critical detail.

Limbacher, James L., comp. and ed. *Film Music; From Violins to Video.* Metuchen, N.J.: Scarecrow Press, 1974.

A reference text consisting of (1) a selection of articles on film music, many from the out-of-print *Film Music Notes,* and (2) cross-indexed listings of films, scores, and composers. The articles, seemingly selected at random, are of varying interest. Section 2 has not been compiled in the tradition of the meticulously accurate Clifford McCarthy *(Film Composers in America),* who has stated in a review of *Film Music,* "The weight of error in this book renders it untrustworthy."

Limbacher, James L. *A Selected List of Recorded Musical Scores from Radio, Television, and Motion Pictures.* Dearborn, Mich.: Dearborn Public Library, 1967.

A good choice of selections; in some cases, however, names of composers and musical directors of individual films are transposed.

London, Kurt. *Film Music.* London: Faber and Faber, 1936. Reprint. New York: Arno Press, 1970.

A thorough historical survey of film music, and an account of the problems of the then contemporary composer, along with an overall probing of the aesthetics of the sound film. This book has aged more gracefully than any other dealing with film music. Important reading for anyone interested in the subject.

Lustig, Milton. *Music Editing for Motion Pictures.* New York: Hastings House, 1980.

Straightforward guide, useful for composers, arrangers, editors, filmmakers, and interested readers. Also contains a very good general discussion of film music. A few photographs of equipment, plus many charts and diagrams. A first on the subject, filling a great need.

Manvell, Roger, and John Huntley. *The Technique of Film Music.*
London: Focal Press, 1957. Revised edition. New York: Hastings House, 1975.
   The most complete review of film music currently available.
Detailed analyses of many scores; numerous statements by
film composers about their own techniques and viewpoints;
chronological listings of outstanding scores and film music
recordings; an excellent bibliography.

McCarty, Clifford. *Film Composers in America.* Glendale, Calif.: By
the author, 1953. Reprint. New York: Da Capo Press, 1972.
   Alphabetically arranged by composers, the book lists,
chronologically, the composers and orchestrators of almost
every American film up to the date of publication. The most
complete, accurate work on film credits yet published. An
updated version by Mr. McCarty would be a worthy addition
to the literature of film music.

Meeker, David. *Jazz in the Movies.* London: British Film Institute,
1972.
   An eclectic mix of 2,239 features and short subjects of many
types, with identification of all jazz musicians involved in the
films, and opinionated, yet valid, résumés of the movies. Index of musicians.

*Music in Film and Television: An International Selective Catalogue,
1964–1974.* Edited by International Music Centre, Vienna.
Paris: UNESCO Press, 1975.
   Listings arranged by composers, film directors, writers, conductors, and performers.

Palmer, Christopher. *Miklos Rozsa: A Sketch of His Life and Work.*
London and Wiesbaden: Breitkopf and Härtel, 1975.
   A musicologist's summation of Rozsa's works for films and
the concert hall, and a brief biography. A short but valuable
study for the music scholar.

Pitts, Michael R., and Louis H. Harrison. *Hollywood on Record:
The Film Stars' Discography.* Metuchen, N.J.: Scarecrow Press,
1980.
   A compilation arranged by performers rather than by films
or composers.

Porcile, François. *Presence de la musique a l'ecran.* Paris: Les Editions du Cerf, 1969.
   A limited reading knowledge of French will suffice for an
understanding of interesting discussions of the aesthetics of
music and criticism of film music. A large section of the book
is devoted to "les bio-filmographies," listing works of many
composers, particularly contemporary ones, along with dis-

cographies and a bibliography. The filmographies are understandable and valuable without any French comprehension.

Prendergast, Roy. *A Neglected Art: A Critical Study of Music in Film.*
New York: New York University Press, 1977.

Prendergast tries to be all things to all readers: aesthetician,
historian, musicologist, even gossipy storyteller. The title
word *neglected* is somewhat negated by the fact that some of
the material in this book has already appeared elsewhere. But
its saving grace is that Prendergast *does* consider film music to
be an art. His sympathetic and empathetic attitude is evident
in his appraisals. The book is also enhanced by sections on
cartoon and avant-garde film music.

Raksin, Ruby. *Mathematics of Motion Picture Synchronization.* Hollywood, Calif.: Pacific Music Papers, 1966.

A technical handbook containing mathematical formulas
pertaining to click tracks, footages, and elapsed time. Valuable
to the professional composer and music editor.

Rubsamen, Walter. *Music in the Dramatic Film.* Washington, D.C.:
United States Information Service, 1956.

A pamphlet, giving elementary explanations of the uses of
background and source music in films, with examples of different types of music cues.

Sabaneev, Leonid L. *Music for the Films.* London: Sir Isaac Pitman and Sons, 1935.

Possibly the earliest book published about music in sound
films, intended as "a handbook for composers and conductors," according to the author. Sabaneev is concerned with
aesthetics and philosophical considerations as well as practi-
cality, but his conclusions are quite generalized. Interesting as
history.

Skiles, Marlin. *Music Scoring for TV and Motion Pictures.* Blue
Ridge Summit, Pa.: Tab Books, 1976.

Practical, informative guide for the composer of film scores.
The text leads from basic musical principles through problems of writing and recording, and finally to the logistics of
copyright and performing-rights income. An appendix includes interviews with six composers.

Skinner, Frank. *Underscore.* New York: Criterion Music Corp.,
1960.

An older, but still practical how-to manual of scoring for
films and filmed television. Some analysis of scores, preceded
by a review of general principles of orchestration and arranging. Valid in its own context, although examples seem somewhat stereotyped. Includes a glossary and many photographs.

Smolian, Steven. *A Handbook of Film, Theater, and Television Music on Record.* New York: Record Undertaker, 1970.
    Two brochures list and index films, record companies' release numbers, and composers. A great deal of information in a small package.

Thomas, Tony, ed. *Film Score: The View from the Podium.* South Brunswick and New York: A. S. Barnes and Co., 1979.
    A varied group of film composers present essays on film music, with introductory sketches by Thomas. Although his actual prose contribution is small, especially compared to that in *Music for the Movies,* the book is still unmistakably Thomas's, and his selection of statements is very good.

Thomas, Tony. *Music for the Movies.* South Brunswick and New York: A. S. Barnes and Co., 1973.
    A well-balanced combination of anecdotal and analytic material; scholarly without being pedantic, enjoyably readable without talking down to its readers. The best of the many survey books on film music.

Ulrich, Allan, ed. *The Art of Film Music: A Tribute to California's Film Composers.* Oakland, Calif.: The Oakland Museum, 1976.
    A catalog of an Oakland Museum symposium, with interviews with participating composers, filmographies, and photographs. Availability is limited, but worth loking for.

Books on Musical Films

Burton, Jack. *The Blue Book of Hollywood Musicals.* Watkins Glen, N.Y.: Century House, 1953.
    A chronological listing of Hollywood musicals and dramatic and Western films with songs. Entries give film titles, studios, directors, stars, and songwriters and their songs; lists are complete up to year of publication. An unfortunately large number of errors, concerning songwriters' credits, however.

Druxman, Michael B. *The Musical: From Broadway to Hollywood.* New York: A. S. Barnes and Co., 1980.
    Critiques of 25 film adaptations of Broadway musical hits, with plot synopses and information about the transition from stage to screen. No new, startling information, but a pleasant mix for browsing. Numerous photographs, of varying quality.

Fordin, Hugh. *The World of Entertainment: Hollywood's Greatest Musicals.* Garden City, N.Y.: Doubleday and Co., 1975.
    A chronicle of the making of the films produced by the Arthur Freed unit at MGM Studios, using a variety of source

materials, including interviews. Includes a most complete filmography of Freed's films.

Harmetz, Aljean. *The Making of The Wizard of Oz.* New York: Alfred A. Knopf, 1977.

An in-depth history of the production of the musical classic, with details of every aspect of the making of *The Wizard.* The book also affords a look into the functioning of a major studio and its music department in the 1930s.

Knox, Donald. *The Magic Factory.* New York: Praeger Publishers, 1973.

Interviews with many people involved in the making of *An American in Paris.* An outgrowth of the American Film Institute's Oral History Project, the book represents oral history as a remarkable tool for film history.

Kobal, John. *Gotta Sing, Gotta Dance: A Pictorial History of Film Musicals.* London: Hamlyn, 1970.

Actually a series of critical articles, rather than a documented history. Somewhat haphazard in organization, but the commentary is amusing. A bibliography, titled "Acknowledgements," is quite complete.

Kreuger, Miles. *The Movie Musical from Vitaphone to 42nd Street.* New York: Dover Publications, 1975.

Utilizing articles and advertisements from *Photoplay* magazine, Kreuger has chronicled the early history of the genre. Nostalgia documentation at its best.

Lerner, Alan Jay. *The Street Where I Live.* New York: W. W. Norton and Co., 1978.

Not a biography, but an account of the production of three of Lerner's successes, two of which are film musicals, *Gigi* and *My Fair Lady* (adapted from the stage version.) A most engaging story of the tribulations of productions on Broadway and in Hollywood.

McVay, Douglas. *The Musical Film.* London: A. Zwemmer; New York: A. S. Barnes and Co., 1967.

A critical, chronological discussion of selected musical films of the years 1927–64. Not intended as history, the book reflects the author's own strong likes and dislikes.

Springer, John. *All Talking, All Singing, All Dancing: A Pictorial History of the Movie Musical.* New York: Citadel Press, 1969.

All pictures, almost. The sparse text, however, does manage to give a good overview of developments and changes in musical-film styles. Some interesting comments on such subgenres as biographical musicals and adaptations of Broadway hits.

Stern, Lee Edward. *The Movie Musical.* New York: Pyramid Communications, 1974.

A worthy attempt to condense almost 50 years of movie history into a scant 144 pages, with some interesting, obscure facts brought to light. Photographs and graphic layout are of poor quality, however.

Taylor, John Russell, and Arthur Jackson. *The Hollywood Musical.* New York: McGraw-Hill, 1971.

In three sections: the first, a series of thoughtful, credible essays by Taylor; the second, filmographies of 275 memorable musicals, plus an index of 1,000 more; the third, "an index of names" that gives quite complete biographies and credits of about 1,100 persons. The best and most accurate book on the subject. The selection of photographs is tasteful, and their number is just adequate.

Thomas, Lawrence B. *The MGM Years.* New York: Columbia House; Arlington House, distributor, 1972.

Almost as much fun as seeing the old films from the golden age of movie musicals. Casts, musical credits, critical evaluations, and spectacular photographs of 40 features. Chapters on sound-track albums, dubbing; helpful listings of songs and songwriters, awards; a discography. A delightful way to be educated in film-music history.

Thomas, Tony. *Harry Warren and the Hollywood Musical.* New York: Citadel Press, 1975.

Anecdotes, pictures, even sheet music, by and of the dean of American motion picture songwriters. A well-deserved tribute, with a wealth of information about the making of many classic musical films.

Valence, Tom. *The American Musical.* New York: A. S. Barnes and Co., 1970.

A small volume, in the form of an encyclopedia. Listings of personalities, with cross-indexed films. A few subject topics are treated, and there are some critical judgments. Quality of biographical material varies: some entries are very complete, others quite sketchy.

Books on Music for Silent Films

Beynon, George W. *Musical Presentation of Motion Pictures.* New York: G. Schirmer, 1921.

Mainly concerned with the building of a musical library and the accompaniment of silent films. Contains biographical sketches and photographs of a few leading movie-music directors.

Borodkin, Maurice M. *Guide to Motion Picture Music.* Los Angeles: By the author, 1928.
    An alphabetical guide to published scores that are suitable for musical accompaniment of silent films. Among composers whose works are mentioned are Axt, Riesenfeld, and Zamecnik.

Classified Catalogue of Sam Fox Publishing Company Motion Picture Music. Cleveland, Ohio: Sam Fox Publishing Co., 1929.
    An index by musical types and titles of musical selections suitable to accompany silent films.

Foort, Reginald. *The Cinema Organ.* 2d ed. Vestal, N.Y.: Vestal Press, 1970.
    Anecdotes and information mixed together, by an author whose enjoyment of the cinema is evident in every page.

Hofman, Charles. *Sounds for Silents.* New York: DBS Publications, 1970.
    Contains a great deal of historical information about musical accompaniments for silents; valuable as a study of the precedents for the scoring of early dramatic sound films. A record is included.

Lang, Edith, and George West. *Musical Accompaniment of Motion Pictures.* New York: Arno Press, 1970. (First published, 1920.)
    A manual for pianists and organists who play for silent films, with suggestions on basic principles of musical interpretation.

Rapee, Erno. *Erno Rapee's Encyclopedia of Music for Pictures.* New York: Belwin, 1924. Reprint. New York: Arno Press, 1970.
    Suggestions for musical accompaniment of silent films. Some commentary on the effects of music on the film audience. Lists of selections, but no scores are included.

―――. *Motion Picture Moods for Pianists and Organists.* New York: Arno Press, 1970. (First published, 1924.)
    A large selection of piano-music scores to accompany silent pictures.

Books on Sound Recording and Reproduction

Cameron, James R. *Sound Motion Pictures: Recording and Reproducing.* 4th ed. Woodmon, Conn.: Cameron Publishing Co., 1941.

Technical manual combining electronic principles with elements of practical operation. First section gives an interesting, nontechnical history of sound recording. Glossary.

Collins, W. H. *The Amateur Filmmaker's Handbook of Sound Sync and Scoring.* Blue Ridge Summit, Pa.: Tab Books, 1974.
A how-to book on the addition of a sound track—dialogue, music, and sound effects—to super-8 mm films and slides.

Cowan, Lester, ed. *Recording Sound for Motion Pictures.* New York: McGraw-Hill Book Co., 1931.
A collection of papers, by several sound engineers and professors of physics, delivered to the Academy of Motion Picture Arts and Sciences School in Sound Fundamentals. Outdated in some respects, but a valuable engineering-level text. Glossary.

Frater, Charles B. *Sound Recording for Motion Pictures.* London: Tantivy Press; New York: A. S. Barnes and Co., 1979.
A text on modern-day recording practices, including the use of tape and film. Sections on editing, re-recording, and transfer of tape to optical sound track.

Frayne, John G., and Halley Wolfe. *Elements of Sound Recording.* New York: John Wiley and Sons, 1949.
Considered the standard work on the subject—pre–solid-state design. Text begins with electronics principles, follows through to chapters on disc, film, and magnetic recording; acoustics; and stereophonic sound. Engineering level.

Mankovsky, V. S. *Acoustics of Studio and Auditoria.* New York: Hastings House, 1971.
Engineering-level treatment of problems of acoustics in concert and studio recording situations.

Motion Picture Sound Engineering. New York: D. Van Nostrand Co., 1938.
Published under the auspices of the Academy of Motion Picture Arts and Sciences to supplant the outdated *Recording Sound,* this text takes into account the technical advances in the intervening years. Text consists of lectures from Academy courses. Included are chapters on equipment and its use, as well as such basics as AC theory, resonant circuits, attenuator networks, and vacuum-tube ampliffirs.

Nisbett, Alec. *The Technique of the Sound Studio, for Radio, Television and Film.* New York: Hastings House, 1972.
Nontechnical manual of many phases of sound recording, including a section of film sound editing.

Overman, Michael. *Understanding Sound, Video, and Film Recording.* Blue Ridge Summit, Pa.: G/L Tab Books, 1978.

A theoretical explanation, rather than a how-to manual, of recording on film and tape. Includes a short history of sound recording and the evolution of video-tape usage.

Pitkin, Walter, and William M. Marston. *The Art of Sound Pictures*. New York and London: D. Appleton and Company, 1930.

A view of the aesthetics and techniques of "the new art," with chapters on sound effects, pp. 194 ff. and sound techniques, pp. 215 ff.

Books with Sections on Music and Sound in Films

Antheil, George. *Bad Boy of Music*. London and New York: Hurst and Blackett, 1947.

Anecdotes, many of them about life in Hollywood, but not a great deal about film music.

Balazs, Bela. *Theory of the Film*. New York: Dover Publications, 1970.

Chapter 16, "Sound," pp. 194–220, is a provocative evaluation of the possibilities inherent in the sound track. Other relevant chapters: "Dialogue," pp. 221–31, "Problem of the Sound Comedy," pp. 232–41, and one about filmed opera, "Musical Forms," pp. 275–82.

Berger, Arthur. *Aaron Copland*. New York: Oxford University Press, 1953.

Contains a brief overview of Copland's film scores.

Bobker, Lee R. *Elements of Film*. New York: Harcourt, Brace and World, 1969.

Discusses many aspects of filmmaking, with emphasis on the relationship of technical and creative processes. Includes sections on sound and music, pp. 97–127 and 143–53.

Brownlow, Kevin. *The Parade's Gone By*. New York: Ballantine Books, 1969.

A few comments on set-side accompaniment of silent filming, pp. 384–88, "The Silents Were Never Silent."

Butler, Ivan. *The Making of a Feature Film: A Guide*. Baltimore, Md.: Penguin Books, 1970.

One chapter devoted to music, pp. 158–66, and one to sound recording and editing, pp. 167–71.

Cameron, Evan, ed. *Sound and the Cinema*. Pleasantville, N.Y.: Redgrave Publishing Co., 1980.

An anthology consisting mainly of the edited proceedings of a symposium called "The Coming of Sound," held at George Eastman House in Rochester in 1973. Chapters by sound engineer James G. Stewart and composer Bernard Herrmann. Stewart's is especially valuable in its information about recording music, speech, and sound effects in the early days of sound films. That by Herrmann (who really had nothing to do with early sound films) is marred by crotchety, inaccurate statements.

Cameron, Ken. *Sound and the Documentary Film*. London: Pitman, 1947.
A handbook for filmmakers, containng a fairly extensive section on sound-recording techniques.

Chase, Donald. *Filmmaking, the Collaborative Art*. Boston: Little, Brown, 1975.
An anthology based on oral histories and seminars conducted by the American Film Institute. Chapter 9, "The Composer," uses material from seminars.

Chavez, Carlos. *Toward a New Music*. New York: W. W. Norton and Co., 1937.
A serious philosophical inquiry, from the composer's viewpoint, into the effects that electronic inventions have had and will have on music. The aesthetic considerations of "The Sound Film," pp. 89–123, are still provocative.

Copland, Aaron. *Our New Music*. New York: Whittlesey House, 1941.
A chapter, "Music in the Film," pp. 260–76, has been deleted from subsequent editions because, as Copland states in the foreword to later editions, "These discussions are now superannuated." But the observations by Copland, who has himself composed excellent film scores, are worth seeking out in the 1941 edition.

Cowie, Peter, ed. *International Film Guide*. New York: A. S. Barnes and Co., 1967–   . (A yearbook.)
Each volume contains a film-music section, with varying subject matter—sometimes a special composer or film, or "Soundtracks of the Year."

Dolan, Robert Emmett. *Music in Modern Media*. New York: G. Schirmer, 1967.
Almost half of this textbook is devoted to techniques of composition and recording of music for films. Examples from works of leading film composers, with scores and cue sheets. The book also includes a section of electronic music and its application to films, pp. 164–73.

Eisenstein, Sergei M. *The Film Form*. New York: Harcourt, Brace and Co., 1949.

Contains a detailed discussion of Meisel's score for *Potemkin*, and of the general use of sound in film. Also includes the statement by Eisenstein, Pudovkin, and Alexandrov on sound film, first published in *Zhizn Iskusstva*, 5 August 1928.

————. *The Film Sense*. New York: Harcourt, Brace and Co., 1942.

It is almost mandatory to read this entire book to grasp Eisenstein's theories about the relationship of sound and image in film. Of particular interest are the detailed analysis (with score and diagrams) of the music in *Alexander Nevsky*, pp. 157–216, the section "Synchronization of the Sense," pp. 69–109, and the ideas about the relationships of color and sound, pp. 113–53.

Ewen, David. *All the Years of American Popular Music*. Englewood Cliffs, N.J.: Prentice-Hall, 1977.

Sections on musical films and the use of songs in motion pictures scattered throughout the book. "The Silent Screen Erupts into Sound," pp. 380–408, and "The Movies, the Radio, and Now Television," pp. 495–508, are of special interest.

Fielding, Raymond, ed. *A Technological History of Motion Pictures and Television*. Berkeley: University of California Press, 1967.

Contains "A History of Sound Motion Pictures," and articles about Augustin Lauste and Joseph T. Tykociner, reprinted from the *Journal of the Society of Motion Picture and Television Engineers*. All are interesting and understandable with even a limited technical background.

Franklin, Harold B. *Sound Motion Pictures, from the Lab to Their Presentation*. Garden City, N.Y.: Doubleday, 1929.

Most of the book deals with the coming of sound, along with an analysis of studio techniques and an operating manual of recording equipment. There are also discussions of speech, hearing, and film music, and some contemporary views of television. Interesting historical reading.

Geduld, Harry M. *The Birth of the Talkies*. Bloomington: Indiana University Press, 1975.

Concerned mostly with the background to the introduction of the Vitaphone, the book touches briefly on music for silent and early sound films.

Gessner, Robert. *The Moving Image*. New York: E. P. Dutton, 1968.

Critical evaluations of films. Chapter 2, "The Auditory Image," pp. 341–88, discusses the use of sound and gives several examples from films of the 1960s.

Gifford, Dennis. *Chaplin.* Garden City, N.Y.: Doubleday and Co., 1947.
A listing, "His Musical Career," gives details of Chaplin's compositions and recordings, including film scores.

Gillett, John, and Roger Manvell. "Music and Film." In *The International Encyclopedia of Film*, pp. 371–74. New York: Crown, 1972.
Excellent survey of film music from the silent era to date of publication. Lists outstanding scores, composers, and musical films.

Gollner, Orville, and George E. Turner. *The Making of King Kong.* New York: A. S. Barnes and Co., 1975.
Contains a brief biographical sketch of Max Steiner, along with details of his work on *King Kong*.

Grau, Robert. *The Theatre of Science.* New York: Benjamin Blom, 1969. (First published, 1914.)
An account of early movie history, including musical accompaniment for silent films. A short section, pp. 331–62, on theater orchestras and organs, and the state of talking and singing films in 1914.

Green, Fitzhugh. *The Film Finds Its Tongue.* New York and London: G. P. Putnam's Sons, 1929.
An adulatory account of the first sound films made by the Warner Brothers, that, in spite of its style, is of historic interest.

Griffith, Richard. *Anatomy of a Motion Picture.* New York: St. Martin's Press, 1959.
The story of the filming of *Anatomy of a Murder*, this book is interesting because of its discussion of a rare occasion when Duke Ellington wrote a film score. Chapter on the film's music, pp. 105–8.

Hampton, Benjamin. *History of the American Film Industry from Its Beginnings to 1931.* New York: Dover Publications, 1970. (First published, 1931.)
Extensive material on early sound films, pp. 362–434.

Happe, L. Bernhard. *Basic Motion Picture Technology.* New York: Hastings House, 1970.
An outline of the technical basis of filmmaking. Chapter 5, "Sound Recording and Reproduction," pp. 146–78; chapter 6, "Studio Production," pp. 206–10, includes paragraphs on sound editing and re-recording.

Huff, Theodore. *Charlie Chaplin. New York: Henry Schuman,*
1951.
   Of the many books on Chaplin's life and films, this is the
only one that offers extensive comments on the use of music
as well as sound effects in his films.

Irving, Ernest, Hans Keller, and Wilfred Mellers. "Film Music."
In *Grove's Dictionary of Music and Musicians,* edited by Eric
Blom. London: Macmillan, 1954.
   The entry, vol. 4, pp. 93–110, give a concise history of film
music, and discusses techniques and aesthetics. A great deal of
information compressed into this entry. Bibliography.

Jacobs, Lewis. *The Movies as Medium.* New York: Farrar, Straus
and Girou, 1970.
   An anthology of critical essays. The section "Sound" includes original material by Jacobs, pp. 243–60, and by Hen-
war Rodakiewicz, pp. 278–8, and reprints of articles by Kurt
Weill and Bela Belazs.

————. *The Rise of the American Film.* New York: Teachers Col-
lege Press, 1968.
   The chapter "Refinements of Technique," pp. 433–45, discusses development of early sound films and problems related
to them.

Jaubert, Maurice. "Music on the Screen." In *Footnotes to the Film,*
edited by Charles Davy, pp. 101–15. New York: Arno Press,
1975. (First published, 1937.)
   Severe but justified criticism of the use of music in some
contemporary films. Regrettably, nothing about Jaubert's own
film scores.

Jinks, William. *The Celluloid Literature: Film in the Humanities.*
New York: Delacorte Press, 1965.
   The book's theme is the relationship of films and literature.
The chapter on the use of sound treats the subject in this
context.

Kinder, Marshe, and Beverle Houston. *Closeup.* New York: Harcourt Brace Jovanovich, 1972.
   Critical essays on films. The section on the use of sound, pp.
51–65, deals mostly with its application in *M* and *Blackmail.*
Many references to and examples of the use of music and
sound in other films are scattered throughout the book.

Kinkle, Roger D. *The Complete Encyclopedia of Popular Music and*
Jazz, 1900–1950. New Rochelle, N. Y.: Arlington House,
1974. Volume 1 contains year-by-year listing of musical
films, with their casts, songs, and songwriters. Volumes 2 and

3 contain biographies of many popular songwriters whose works have been performed in films.

Knight, Arthur. *The Liveliest Art.* New York: Macmillan Co., 1957. Revised edition, 1978.

Sections on the advent of sound and the wise use of the new medium by Mamoulian, Welles, and others, pp. 124–63. Some obscure facts about music and sound throughout the book.

Kracauer, Siegfried. *Theory of Film.* London: Oxford University Press, 1960.

Analysis of films according to the author's rationale. Sections on sound and music, pp. 102–56. Included is a review of existing theories of the relationship of sound and film image.

Lambert, Constant. *Music Ho! A Study of Music in the Decline.* New York: Charles Scribner's Sons, 1936.

A cynical view of music in general. The chapter "Mechanical Music and the Cinema," pp. 256–68, gives some unflattering observations on films and film music; the points made are not too anachronistic. Predictions are more accurate than those in most books of this period.

Levant, Oscar. *The Memoirs of an Amnesiac.* New York: G. P. Putnam's Sons, 1965.

Anecdotes and witty observations about movies and life in Hollywood are scattered throughout the book.

———. *A Smattering of Ignorance.* New York: Doubleday, Doran and Co., 1940.

The chapter "A Cog in the Wheel," pp. 89–146, is a devastating and most accurate account of what it was like to work in a Hollywood studio music department in the 1930s. The book also contains some comments concerning film music techniques that remain valid today.

———. *The Unimportance of Being Oscar.* New York: G. P. Putnam's Sons, 1968.

Anecdotes and incisive observations of movies, music, and Hollywood, as in previous Levant books.

Limbacher, James L. *Four Aspects of the Film.* New York: Brussel and Brussel, 1969.

A well-researched book that treats film production historically rather than as a how-to manual. The section devoted to an overview of the development of sound-recording techniques, pp. 197–232, also lists outstanding early sound films.

Lindgren, Ernest. *The Art of the Film.* New York: Macmillan Co., 1963.

This survey of film techniques includes a discussion of the

aesthetics of sound and music, along with numberous examples of the use of each in specific films, pp. 97–116 and 141–54.

Lindsay, Vachel. *The Art of the Moving Picture.* New York: Macmillan Co., 1922.
A scathing put-down of *all* musical accompaniment of films in chapter 14, pp. 189–206. Says Lindsay, "I suggest suppressing the orchestra entirely and encouraging the audience to talk about the film."

Mayer, Michael F. *The Film Industries.* New York: Hastings House, 1973.
Discusses the business aspects of film music, pp. 191–95, including copyright, licensing, etc., from the viewpoint of the film producer and distributor.

MacCann, Richard Dyer. *Film, a Montage of Theories.* New York: Dutton, 1966.
An anthology. Includes a chapter by René Clair, "The Art of Sound," pp. 38–44, and "Sight and Sound," pp. 45–52, by Gavin Lambert.

McClelland, Paul. *The Unkindest Cuts.* New York: A. S. Barnes and Co., 1972.
A book about sequences that were edited out of films, including a chapter about musical numbers that were cut from films and, in some instances, inserted in subsequent movies, pp. 157–73.

Manvell, Roger. *Film.* Harmondsworth, England: Penguin Books, 1950.
Discussions of the aesthetics of sound, somewhat like those in the more recent *The Film and the Public.*

————. *The Film and the Public.* Harmondsworth, England: Penguin Books, 1958.
Section on the aesthetics of sound and music, along with an analysis of Eisenstein's writings about sound in *The Film Sense,* pp. 54–83.

Mattfield, Julius, ed. *Variety Musical Cavalcade: Musical-Historical Review, 1920–1969.* Englewood Cliffs, N.J.: Prentice-Hall, 1971.
Films receive much attention throughout this history of musical entertainment and yearly summary of America's most popular songs.

Milhaud, Darius. *Notes without Music.* London: Dennis Dobson, 1952.
Brief chapter on Milhaud's own limited work in films.

Miller, Maud M., ed. *Winchester's Screen Encyclopedia.* London: Winchester Publications, 1948.
   Articles about and listings of notable film music of the period, by Muir Mathieson and John Huntley.

Milne, Tom. *Rouben Mamoulian.* Bloomington: University of Indiana Press, 1969.
   The book is noteworthy because it gives details of the director's pioneering in audio effects in film, and of his work in musical films.

Minnelli, Vincente, with Hector Arce. *I Remember It Well.* Garden City, N.Y.: Doubleday and Co., 1974.
   The famed director's biography, with extensive sections on his outstanding musical films, including *An American in Paris* and *Gigi.*

Myers, Rollo H. *Twentieth Century Music.* London: J. Calder, 1961.
   Contains a concise historical review of film music, with examples of silent and sound film scores, and a list of outstanding film scores.

Naumberg, Nancy. *We Make the Movies.* New York: W. W. Norton and Co., 1937.
   A chapter on film scoring, by Max Steiner, pp. 216–38, and one on sound recording, by Nathan Levinson, a pioneer in electronic engineering in films, pp. 173–93.

Pasternak, Joseph. *Easy the Hard Way.* London: W. H. Allen, 1951.
   An informal biography. Scattered throughout the book are many anecdotes about the making of musical films.

Previn, André, and Antony Hopkins. *Music Face to Face.* London: Hamish Hamilton, 1971.
   Conversation between the two authors about their lives and various facets of music, including film music. The talk is thoughtful, sometimes witty, often opinionated.

Pudovkin, V. I. *Film Techniques* and *Film Acting.* (One-volume edition.) London: Vision Press, 1949 and 1954.
   Pudovkin discusses "sound as a means of expression" in film, and his problems in making his first sound film. Noteworthy sections: "Asynchronism as a principle of sound," pp. 183–93, "Rythmic problems of my first sound film," pp. 194–202, and "Dual rhythm of sound and image," pp. 308–16.

Riesenfeld, Hugo. "Music and Motion Pictures." In *The Motion Picture and Its Economic and Social Aspects.* Philadelphia: The

American Academy of Political and Social Science (Annals, November 1926, vol. 128.)

Résumé of the role of film music up to (and including) the introduction of Vitaphone. Interesting for glowing predictions, most of which, unfortunately, did not come true.

Roberts, Kenneth H., and Win Sharples, Jr. *A Primer for Filmmaking*. New York: Bobbs-Merrill Co., 1971.

Although this book is basically a manual for film production, the chapter "The Audial Image," pp. 339–69, gives a serious evaluation of the sound track's aesthetic meaning. A short history of film sound introduces examples of effective use of both sound and music. The technical section on sound and music editing and sound mixing, pp. 430–69, is clear, complete, and instructive.

Rosenberg, Bernard, and Harry Silverstein. *The Real Tinsel*. New York: The Macmillan Co., 1970.

Interviews with filmmakers, including composer Max Steiner, pp. 387–98, and sound engineer Douglas Shearer, pp. 373–84. Concise and informative.

Scotland, John. *The Talkies*. London: Crosby Lockwood, 1930.

An early attempt to explain the techniques of making sound films. The last chapter, pp. 184–94, contains quotes from contemporary newspapers and magazines evaluating sound films. Interesting text and photographs.

Seldes, Gilbert. *An Hour with the Movies and the Talkies*. Philadelphia: J. P. Lippincott, 1929.

An early critical assessment of the advent of sound and its impact on the audience. Brief, but of historical interest.

Smith, John. *Jean Vigo*. London: November Books, 1972.

Valuable to the study of film music for the excellent, detailed explanation of the work of Maurice Jaubert in composing the score—one of the first to use *musique concrete* techniques—for *Zéro de Conduite*.

Smith, Julia. *Aaron Copland: His Work and Contribution to American Music*. New York: E. P. Dutton and Co., 1955.

Includes a musicologist's analysis of Copland's film scores.

Spottiswoode, Raymond. *Film and Its Techniques*. Berkeley: University of California Press, 1950.

A production manual for filmmakers, particularly applicable to documentaries. Sections on sound recording and editing, pp. 275–336, present technical details in a fairly simple fashion. The use of stock (library) music is touched on very briefly.

————. *A Grammar of the Film*. Berkeley: University of California Press, 1950.

> The book analyzes film by considering various factors as grammatical parts of the language of film. Speech, sound, and music represent a great portion of the material dissected, pp. 48–50, 114–16, 231–40, and 185–97.

Stephenson, Ralph, and J. R. Debroix. *The Cinema as Art*. Harmondsworth, England: Penguin Books, 1965.

> The book deals with film aesthetics. The chapter "The fifth dimension, sound," pp. 174–200, gives an in-depth analysis of the techniques involved in the creative use of sound and music. One of the best of all critical discussions of sound as a vital aspect of film.

Sternfeld, Frederic W. "Film Music." In *Harvard Dictionary of Music*, edited by Willi Appel. Cambridge, Mass.: Harvard University Press, Belknap Press, 1969.

> Short overview of film music, with list of notable scores and bibliography, pp. 314–15.

Stokowski, Leopold. *Music for All of Us*. New York: Simon and Schuster, 1943.

> In one chapter, pp. 241–47, Stokowski tells what film music *can* do, citing examples from *Fantasia*.

Sutak, Ken. *The Great Motion Picture Soundtrack Robbery*. Hamden, Conn.: The Shoe String Press, 1976.

> Discusses copyright protection and the pirating of sound tracks and sound-track albums, in highly technical legal terminology.

Sutro, John, ed. *Diversion: Twenty-two Authors on the Lively Arts*. London: Max Parrish, 1950.

> An anthology of essays. "The Celluloid Plays a Tune," by Alan Rawsthorne, pp. 25–34, is a generalized overview of film music. A chapter by Robert Helpmann, "The Orchestration of Movement," pp. 198–206, discusses ballet in films.

The Technique of Motion Picture Production: Papers Presented at a Symposium at the 51st Semi-Annual Convention of the Society of Motion Picture Engineers, Hollywood, California. New York: Interscience Publishers, 1944.

> Papers include "Re-recording," by L. T. Goldsmith, p. 43, with a good bibliography; "Production Sound Recording," by Homer G. Trasker, p. 54, and "Pre-scoring and Scoring," by Bernard Brown, p. 65. Good descriptions of studio practices at the time.

Thomson, Virgil. *The State of Music*. New York: Random House, 1962.

Not a great deal about films; short reference to his own film-music work.

Tiomkin, Dimitri, with Prosper Buranelli. *Please Don't Hate Me.* Garden City, N.Y.: Doubleday, 1961.

Most of this lightweight but highly amusing book deals with the composer's life and career in Hollywood.

Vidor, King. *King Vidor on Film Making.* New York: David McKay, 1972.

Short section on film musicals, notable for Vidor's account of his part in the shooting of "Over the Rainbow."

Walker, Alexander. *The Shattered Silents.* London: Elm Tree Books, 1978.

Although the author states that the book covers a part of film history—the transition from silents to sound—not documented before, much of the material duplicates that in Geduld's *The Birth of the Talkies.* And Walker's folksy literary style is less readable than Geduld's restrained scholarship.

Warner, Jack, with Dean Jennings. *My First Hundred Years in Hollywood.* New York: Random House, 1965.

Valuable to the study of sound-recording history for Warner's description of the making of early sound films.

Watts, Stephen. *Behind the Screen.* London: Barker, 1938.

Contains short essays by Herbert Stothart, on the value of good music in films, and Douglas Shearer, who gives an elementary introduction into sound recording.

Whitaker, Rod. *The Language of Film.* Englewood Cliffs, N.J.: Prentice-Hall, 1970.

An exploration of film structure, more explanatory than critical. Includes a section called "The Audio Content," pp. 99–112.

Wilk, Max. *They're Playing Our Song.* New York: Atheneum, 1973.

Profiles of several songwriters, many of whom discuss the writing of film songs, including "Over the Rainbow," "Lullaby of Broadway," and "Thanks for the Memory."

Winkler, Max. *A Penny from Heaven.* New York: Appleton-Century-Crofts, 1951.

Folksy, anecdotal account of many years in the music business, including the story of compiling and furnishing music cue sheets to silent-movie theaters. (Winkler claims to have invented the cue sheet.) Parts of this book were printed in *Films in Review,* December 1951, simultaneously with the book publication.

Wysotsky, Michael Z. *Wide Screen Cinema and Stereophonic Sound.* New York: Hastings House, 1970.
An explanation of various innovative projection systems, along with a description of the stereo system usually used with each. "The technology of stereo sound for film," pp. 88–151, is quite comprehensive. Fairly technical.

Periodical Articles about Music and Sound in Film

Adams, Stanley. "Music and Motion Pictures." *ASCAP Today* 1, no. 2 (June 1967): A.
An editorial about the musical taste of the film audience, and the relationship of the songwriter to that audience.

Alpert, Hollis. "Through a Screen, Darkly." *Saturday Review*, 24 August 1963, p. 35.
Raises serious questions about English-language dubbing of foreign films.

Altman, Charles F. "The American Film Musical." *Wide Angle* 2, no. 2 (1978): 10–17.
An analysis of the structure of movie musicals, based mainly on that of *Gigi*.

Alwyn, William. "Composing for the Screen." *Films and Filming*, March 1959, p. 9.
Good but brief discussion of the purposes and function of film music.

American Record Guide
The magazine contains occasional reviews of sound-track records, usually by Mark Koldys.

Antheil, George. "Hollywood Composer." *Atlantic Monthly*, February 1940, pp. 160–67.
An interesting portrait of an anonymous film composer.

———. "Music Takes a Screen Test." *The American Scholar*, no. 3, 1937, pp. 354–64.
Provocative ideas.

Arnold, Malcolm. "Film Music." *Recorded Sound*, April 1965, pp. 328–34.
Transcript of a lecture given to the Institute of Recorded Sound.

Arvey, Violet. "Present Day Films and How They Are Made Possible." *Etude*, January 1931, p. 16.
Interesting historically; a view of contemporary practices.

Austin, Cecil. "Cinema Music." *Music and Letters,* April 1924, pp. 177–91.
    A scathing diatribe against silent-film music scores, with especially unkind words about D. W. Griffith's motion picture music scores.

Bach, Steven. "The Hollywood Idiom." *Arts Magazine,* December 1967, pp. 16–17.
    About studio musicians.

Bakshy, Alexander. "The Movie Scene: Notes on Sound and Silence." *Theatre Arts Magazine,* February 1929, pp. 97–107.
    A deprecation of sound films.

Beatty, Jerome. "Norma Shearer's Noisy Brother." *American Magazine,* May 1937, pp. 26–27 +
    The title is misleading: the article gives a great many facts about studio sound recording.

Becker, Leon. "Synthetic Sound and Abstract Image." *Hollywood Quarterly* 1, no. 1 (October 1945): 95–96.
    Describes several innovative filmmaking processes, including the work of James and John Whitney.

Beckley, P. V. "Divas in Movieland." *Opera News,* 19 December 1964, pp. 8–13.
    About opera films and their stars.

Behlmer, Rudy. "Erich Korngold." *Films in Review,* February 1967, pp. 86–100.
    A long career article; very little musical analysis.

Bender, Albert K. "Max Steiner." *Film Music Notebook* 1 (Fall 1974): 5–11.
    A career overview, with a filmography.

Berg, Charles Merrell. "Cinema Sings the Blues." *Cinema Journal* 17, no. 2 (Spring 1978): 1–12
    A critique of the use of jazz in certain specific films.

Bernstein, Elmer. "The Aesthetics of Film Scoring." *Film Music Notebook* no. 1 (1978): 22–27.
    Bernstein describes his pronouncement as "highly personal," which it is, but it is also valid.

———. "The Annotated Friedkin." *Film Music Notebook* 1 (Winter 1974): 10–16.
    Clever, valid "footnotes" (i.e., refutations) to William Friedkin's American Film Institute seminar remarks about the music of *The Exorcist.*

———. "Bronislaw Kaper Interview." *Film Music Notebook* (1978): 12–28.

Witty comments by Kaper on his film work and present involvement with symphony associations. Includes a filmography.

————. "A Conversation with Daniele Amfitheatrof." *Film Music Notebook,* Summer 1975, pp. 14–22.
The composer's views on his career, in answer to Bernstein's short, direct questions.

————. "A Conversation with David Raksin." Part 1, *Film Music Notebook* no. 2 (1976): 14–21; part 2, vol. 2, no. 3 (1976): 9–18.
Traces Raksin's career, and includes opinions on various aspects of film music.

————. "A Conversation with George Roy Hill." *Film Music Notebook* 1 (Winter 1974–75): 17–25.
A dialogue in which the director gives his views on the use of music in films. Sometimes Bernstein's questions are longer than Hill's answers.

————. "A Conversation with Henry Mancini." *Film Music Notebook,* 4 no. 1 (1978): pp. 9–21.
A career interview, with a fimography and list of Mancini's many awards.

————. "A Conversation with Jerry Goldsmith." *Film Music Notebook* 3, no. 2 (1977): 18–30.
Review of Goldsmith's career and discussion of his writing style.

————. "A Conversation with John Addison." *Film Music Notebook* 3 (1977), no. 3: 18–32.
A review of Addison's career and discussion of the problems of writing for films.

————. "A Conversation with John Green." Part 1, *Film Music Notebook,* 2, no. 4, (1976): 9–21; part 2, vol. 3, no. 1 (1977): 15–31.
The interview concentrates on Green's early career and his years as head of the MGM music department. Part 1 also includes a biography and filmography.

————. "A Conversation with Leo Shuken." *Film Music Notebook,* Spring 1975, pp. 14–26.
Review of Shuken's career, and discussion of the many composers with whom he worked.

————. "A Conversation with Robert Russell Bennett." *Film Music Notebook* 2, no. 1 (1976): 16–25.
Covers Bennett's career, including his work in theater and films.

————. "Film Composers vs. the Studios." *Film Music Notebook* 2, no. 1, 1976, pp. 31–39.

An explanation of the Composers and Lyricists Guild of America's lawsuit against the motion picture producers.

————. "Interview with Hugo Friedhofer." *Film Music Notebook* 1 (Fall 1974): 12–21.
Friedhofer discusses his own films and early scores by other composers.

————. "On Film Music." *Journal of the University Film Association,* Fall 1976, pp. 7–9.
Transcript of a lecture given at a UFA conference. Short, to-the-point résumé of the functions of film music.

————. "What Ever Happened to Great Movie Music?" *High Fidelity,* July 1972, pp. 55–58. (Reprinted in *Crossroads to the Cinema,* Douglas Brode, ed. Boston: Holbrook Press, 1975.)
An evaluation of the changes that occurred in film music during the 1960s and 1970s.

Bolger, Ray. "*The Wizard of Oz* and the Golden Era of the American Musical Film." *American Cinematographer 59, no. 2 (February 1978): 190–94.*
Excerpts from several interviews with Bolger, about his work in the classic film and other musicals.

Bomba, Raymond. "What Does a Sound Editor Do?" *Cinemeditor,* Summer 1971, pp. 9–11.
Lucid explanation by a veteran in his craft.

Borneman, Ernest J. "Sound Rhythm and the Film." *Sight and Sound,* November 1934, p. 66.
An evaluation of the sound track.

Broeck, John. "Music of the Fears." *Film Comment* 12, no. 5 (September–October 1976): 56–60.
An analysis of some of Bernard Herrmann's scores. Includes a list of his music.

Brown, Royal S. "Changing the Score." *American Film* 2, n. 6 (April 1977): 62–63.
About new films scored by younger composers.

Canby, Edward Tatnall. "Music for Background." *Saturday Review of Literature,* 8 January 1944, p. 29.
More about literature than about music.

Caps, John. "A Correspondence with Miklos Rozsa." *Film Music Notebook* 2, no. 1 (1976): 2–5.
A discussion of musical aesthetics.

————. "The John Barry Triptych." *Film Music Notebook* 2, no. 4 (1976): 6–8.
A review of some ofBarry's scores.

————. "John Williams—Scoring the Film Whole." *Film Music Notebook* 2, no. 3 (1976): 19–25.
Cinematic analysis ofWilliams's scores.

————. "The Lyricism of Mancini." *Film Music Notebook* 3, no. 2 (1977): 12–17.
Critique of Mancini's style.

————. "Serial Music of Jerry Goldsmith." *Film Music Notebook* 2, no. 1 (1976): 26–30.
Analysis of several scores, not overly technical.

————. "The Third Language: The Art of Film Music." *Film Music Notebook* Spring 1975, pp. 10–13.
The function and aesthetics of movie music.

Care, Ross. "Cynesymphony: Music and Animation at the Disney Studio, 1928–42." *Sight and Sound*, Winter 1976–77, pp. 40–44.
Excellent report on the teamwork of musicians and visual technicians in Disney cartoons, including shorts that anticipated *Fantasia*.

————. "The Film Music of Leigh Harline." *Film Music Notebook* 3, no. 2 (1977): 32–48.
Extensive, very complete review of the composer's work.

Churchill, Sir Winston. "Everybody's Language." *Collier's,* 26 October 1935, p. 24 + .
Essay about the influence of sound on the style of Charlie Chaplin.

"Cinema Music." *Music Journal,* May 1968–70.
A column that appeared fairly regularly for about two years.

Comolli, Jean Louis. "Busby Berkeley: Dancing Images." *Cahiers du Cinéma in English.* No. 2, 1966, p. 26.
A short critique, plus a rare interview with Berkeley, by Patrick Brion and Rene Gilson, and a filmography by Ralph Crandall.

"Confessions of a Film Composer: Victor Young." *Music Journal,* September 1956, p. 16.
An interview with Young when his career was at its height.

Considine, Shaun, "The Music behind the Dialogue Steps Out." *After Dark,* October 1973, pp. 45–47.
Explores two topics: the use of records in films, and the renewed popularity of sound-track albums from older films.

Cook, Page. "Film Scores of Bernard Herrmann." *Films in Review,* September 1967, pp. 398–412.
A review of Herrmann's film work.

Copland, Aaron. "A Tip to Moviegoers: Take Off Those Ear-muffs." *New York Times Magazine*, 6 November 1949, pp. 28–32.
   Very good suggestions about listening to film scores more carefully and intelligently.

Creston, Paul. "Music and Mass Media." *Music Educators Journal*, April 1970, pp. 35–36.
   A thoughtful article about composing for films and other media.

Curley, Joseph. "Elmer Bernstein: How Rock Has Rolled over Film Scoring *Millimeter* 8, no. 8 (August 1980): 134–39.
   The composer discusses his recent scores and trends in film music.

———. "A Few Easy Pieces." *Millimeter* 7, no. 4 (April 1979): 35–36.
   In *profile* form, interviews with Bill Conti and Jerry Goldsmith about their careers.

———. "Nobody Does It Better." *Millimeter*, 7, no. 6 (June 1979): pp. 26–30 +.
   In the *profile* format, Henry Mancini and Marvin Hamlisch evaluate their own film work.

———, and Ric Gentry. "Commercial Composers Choose Up Sides." *Millimeter* 8, no. 7 (July 1980): 94–111.
   About trends in songwriting and composing for filmed commercials, with interviews with writers and technicians.

Dale, S. S. "Contemporary Cello Concerti: Korngold and Pende-recki." *The Strad* 87, no. 1036 (August 1976): 277–89.
   A reevaluation and favorable critique of the Korngold Con-certo, first heard in the film *Devotion*. Dale refutes the carping criticism of Andre Previn et al.

———. "Contemporary Cello Concerti: Miklos Rozsa, Hendrik Herman Badings." *The Strad* 87, no. 1041 (January 1977): 735–45.
   Dale discusses Rozsa's work, both for film and for the con-cert hall, aptly delineating the relationship of each to his en-tire career.

Darby, Ken. "Letter," and "Al Newman Biography and Filmog-raphy." *Film Music Notebook* 2 no. 2 (1976): 3–8.
   The biography is mostly about Newman's early career.

Daugherty, F. J. "Twenty Years of Sound." *Christian Science Monitor Magazine*, 3 August 1946, pp. 8–9.
   A nontechnical but thorough review of the development of sound films.

"David Raksin Biography and Filmography." *Film Music Notebook* 2. no. 3 (1976): 3–8.
Includes short introductory comment by Elmer Bernstein.

Deutsch, Adolph. "Three Strangers." *Hollywood Quarterly* 1: 214–23.
An excellent account of the relationships of composer, film producer, and director.

De Vore, Nicholas, "Film Music Attains to Artistic Stature." *Musician,* November 1946, pp. 150–51.
A review of the work of Korngold, Alexander Tansman, and other film composers.

Doeckel, Ken. "Miklos Rozsa." *Films in Review,* November 1963, pp. 536–48.
A biography: includes a filmography.

"Edison's Kinetophonic Theater." *Hobbies,* January 1953, p. 152 +.
A nontechnical description of Edison's sound films.

Elley, Derek. "The Film Composer: 4, Jerry Goldsmith." *Films and Filming,* May and June 1979, pp. 20–24 and 20–24.
An interview/review of Goldsmith's career. Includes a filmography.

———. "The Film Composer: 3, John Williams." *Films and Filming,* July and August 1978, pp. 20–24 and 3–33.
An interview about Williams's film work, and other facets of his career.

Epstein, Dave A. "Backstage with the Film Composer." *Etude,* February 1953, p. 19 +.
An interview with Dimitri Tiomkin, containing a good description of Hollywood studio practices at the time.

Everson, William K. "The History of the Musical." In *Film Review, 1957–1958,* edited by F. Maurice Speed, pp. 17–21.
A section in a yearbook of films. A thorough discussion of the evolution of the film musical and its varying styles through the years.

Feather, Leonard. "From Pen to Screen." *International Musician,* September 1968–1973.
A column, appearing more or less regularly, commenting on various aspects of film music.

Ferguson, Stanley. "Gone with the Soundtrack: Pit Orchestras." *New Republic,* 30 March 1942, pp. 426–27.
Very good description of the effects of sound on live music (and musicians) in theaters.

Fiedel, Robert. "The Filmharmonic." *American Film* 3, no. 6 (April 1978): 64–65.
   The author deplores the lack of concert performances of film music.

———. "Saving the Score." *American Film* 3, no. 1 (October 1977): 32–71.
   About the need for preserving film scores and related material.

"Film Music." *American Cinematographer,* April 1962.
   Pointers on film music for filmmakers with 16 mm equipment.

"Film Music." *Music Review,* beginning August 1948.
   A column, issued rather irregularly.

"Film Music." *Musical Times,* beginning August 1955.
   A column, issued fairly regularly until 1960.

"Film Music of the Quarter." *Hollywood Quarterly,* beginning 1945.
   A series of article/columns, usually written by Lawrence Morton, appearing in volumes 1, 2, 3, and 4. Very good reviews and analyses of then-current films and scores.

"The Film Musical Golden 13." *Action* 9, no. 3, (May–June 1974): 4–9.
   As part of a special edition of *Action* devoted to the film musical, the results are announced of a poll of 100 film critics who chose all-time great musicals.

Film Music Notes
   Film Music Notes was published from October 1941 until Fall and Winter 1957–58. (The name of the magazine was changed: first, in 1951, to *Film Music,* and again in 1956, to *Film and TV Music,* but the format remained essentially the same throughout the publication years.) *Film Music Notes* appeared originally in modest mimeographed form. Later, facsimiles of scores and photographs were added. The articles ranged from breezy "news" columns to scholarly analyses of many significant film scores. If copies of the magazine are available to the reader/researcher, it is suggested that he/she allot sufficient time to peruse all accessible issues. Not only will one find a wealth of material on every aspect of film music in the 1940s and 1950s; the reader will gain, between the lines, a chance to glimpse into the workings of the motion picture studio and the way in which films were scored in that memorable era.

Ford, Peter. "History of Sound Recording. IV: Motion Picture and Television Sound Recording." *Recorded Sound* 2, no. 12 (October 1963): 146–54.
   Part of a thorough, scholarly six-part series.

Forrest, David. "From Score to Screen." *Hollywood Quarterly* 1, no. 2 (January 1946): 224–29.
   The problems of music recording and dubbing reviewed by one of Hollywood's most highly regarded sound engineers.

Franchere, L. C. "The Rebirth of Music." *Catholic World*, December 1951, pp. 36–39.
   An article with a debatable view: that mechanized means of music, such as the recorded sound track, have caused a renaissance of interest in better music.

Frankenstein, Alfred. "Franz Waxman's Music for *The Silver Chalice,"Film Music Notebook,* Spring 1975, pp. 27–35.
   An eminent musicologist's straightforward analysis, in understandable terms.

"Franz Waxman." *Film Music Notebook,* Spring 1975, pp. 6–9.
   A career overview, with a filmography.

Gabriel, Jack P., and Stanley Kauffman. "Films: To Dub or Not to Dub." *Theatre Arts Magazine,* October 1961, p. 20 + .
   Convincing arguments for and against English-language dubbing of foreign films.

Gallez, Douglas W. "The Prokofieff-Eisenstein Collaboration." *Cinema Journal* 17, no. 2 (Spring 1978): 13–35.
   Examination of Prokofieff's and Eisenstein's work together on *Alexander Nevsky* and *Ivan the Terrible,* with notes on their basic philosophies about the function of music in films.

————. "Satie's *Entr'acte:* A Model of Film Music." *Cinema Journal* 16, no. 1 (Fall 1971): 36–50.
   Although Gallez carefully analyzes Satie's music score, the fact (as he admits) that he has not viewed and heard the version postsynchronized in 1968 detracts from the potential value of the article.

————. "Theories of Film Music." *Cinema Journal* 9, no. 2 (Spring 1979): 40–47.
   Reviews the theories of several authors and suggests a new approach to criticism of film music.

Galling, Dennis. "Arthur Freed." *Films in Review* (November 1964): 521–44.
   A career overview, a critique of several of Freed's films, and a filmography.

Gardner, Paul. "Bob Fosse." *Action* 9, no. 3 (May–June 1974): 22–27.
> An evaluation of the choreographer/director's work, mostly about *Cabaret*.

Gold, Ernest. "Notes from the Cutting Room." *Opera News*, 23 December 1961, pp. 8–13.
> Explains some of the problems encountered by the film composer.

Goldbeck, Frederick. "Current Chronicle: France." *Musical Quarterly*, vol. 36, no. 3 (July 1950): 457–60.
> Rather esoteric article about music and film in France.

Gomery, Douglas. "Tri-Ergon, Tobis-Klangfilm, and the Coming of Sound." *Cinema Journal*. 16, no. 1 (Fall 1976): 51–61.
> The role played by the German recording and reproduction patents in the coming of sound to films.

Green, Stanley. "Richard Rodgers' Filmusic." *Films in Review*, October 1965, pp. 8–13.
> Good overview, especially of the composer's early films.

———. "Hammerstein's Film Career." *Films in Review*, February 1957, pp. 68–77.
> Interesting, similar to the article about Rodgers.

Haggin, B. H. "Music for the Documentary Film." *Nation*, 15 February 1940, p. 194.
> The function of music in the genre.

Hammond, Richard. "Pioneers of Movie Music." *Modern Music*, 7, no. 3 (March/April 1931): 35–38.
> A good review of early film music; of interest as part of a special edition of the magazine, "Music and the Machine," devoted to the relationship of music to film, radio, and phonograph recordings.

"The Handwritten Soundtrack." *Music Educators Journal*, November 1968, p. 114+.
> Extensive review of the subject.

Harvey, Steven. "Eine Kleiser Rockmusik." *Film Comment* 14, no. 4 (July/August 1978): 15–16
> A profile of Randal Kleiser, director of *Grease*, and some comments about rock music films.

Hauduroy, Jean François. "Writing for Musicals: Comden and Green Interview." *Cahiers du Cinéma in English*, no. 2, 1966, pp. 43–50.
> Betty Comden and Adolph Green discuss their film work and writing methods; a filmography by Patrick Brion.

Haun, Harry, and George Raborn. "Max Steiner." *Films in Review,* June/July 1961, pp. 338–51.
A review of the composer's career, with a filmography.

Hendricks, Gordon. "Film Music Comes of Age." *Films in Review,* June 1952, pp. 22–27.
Considers changes in film scoring in past few years.

Hentoff, Nat. "Movie Music Comes into Its Own." *Reporter,* 12 June 1958, pp. 28–30.
A review of recent trends.

Herrmann, Bernard. "From Soundtrack to Disc." *Saturday Review of Literature,* 27 September 1947, p. 47.
A statement of Herrmann's views on trends in film music.

Hickman, C. S. "Dimitri Tiomkin's Method of Composition." *Music Journal,* April 1955, pp. 46–47.
An interview with the composer about his film career.

———. "MGM's Music Department." *Music Journal,* July 1954, 31+.
Interesting article about a famous Hollywood institution.

———. "Music School for Movies." *Music Journal,* June 1954, pp. 18–19.
About film-music courses at the University of Southern California.

Higham, Charles. "George Sidney." *Action* 9, no. 3, (May/June 1974): 17–23.
An evaluation of the director's films, with emphasis on the musicals he directed.

Hopkins, Antony. "Music." *Sight and Sound,* December 1949, p. 23; March 1950, pp. 32–33; May 1950, p. 127.
Discussions of recent film music.

———. "Music: Congress at Florence." *Sight and Sound* August 1950, pp. 243–44.
Report on the conference and discussion of major papers that were read there.

———. "Music: Letter from an Unknown Critic." *Sight and Sound,* February 1951, p. 416.
Critique of several new film scores.

———. "The Music of Copland." *Sight and Sound,* December 1950, p. 336.
Very good musical analysis.

———, and Lawrence Morton. "Orchestration Run Riot?" *Sight and Sound,* May 1951.
Review of recent trends in instrumental writing.

Horning, Joseph. "Shooting a Live Symphony Orchestra." *American Cinematographer* 59, no. 3 (March 1978): 264–65.
    Detailed description of camera placement, use of multiple cameras and microphones, etc., in filming a concert.

Huntley, John. "Film Music." *Sight and Sound,* January 1944, pp. 90–93.
    Intelligent review of developments in film music up to time of publication. A letter from Darrel Catling, in *Sight and Sound,* May 1944, cites examples of film scores Huntley omitted.

———. "Film Music Orchestras." *Penguin Film Review,* no. 5, January 1948, pp. 14–18.
    About the complements of studio orchestras, and symphonic orchestras that have appeared in feature films.

———. "Music in Films." *Musical Times,* December 1957, pp. 662–63.
    About the aesthetics of film music.

———. "Notes on Film Music." *Penguin Film Review,* no. 1, August 1946, pp. 35–37.
    Critique of several current film scores.

———. "The Sound Track." *Sight and Sound,* various issues, 1951–53.
    Short, thoughtful article/columns. Subjects include the MGM studio orchestra, music in Chaplin's films, and the role of sound effects and music in films.

Irving, Ernest. "Music and the Film Script." *Film Music Notebook,* Summer 1975, pp. 10–13.
    Transcript of a talk given to the (British) Screenwriters' Association, intended, the author states, "only to sow the seed of reflection."

"It All Started with 'Ramona,'" *ASCAP Today,* no. 1, 1971, pp. 32–33.
    Examples of theme songs, particularly those of silent films.

"It's a Whole New Scene for Film Cleffers: Arthur Hamilton." *Variety,* 7 April 1971.
    Interview about changing trends in the hiring of songwriters for films.

Jablonski, Edward. "Filmusicals." *Films in Review,* February 1955, pp. 56–61.
    A summary of the history of musical films.

———, and Milton A. Caine. "Gershwin's Movie Music," *Films in Review,* October 1951, pp. 23–28.

A career article, concentrating on the composer's movie musicals, with a filmography.

————, and William R. Sweigert. "Harold Arlen." *Films in Review*, December 1962, pp. 605–14.
About Arlen's films. Includes a filmography.

Jacobs, Jack. "Alfred Newman." *Films in Review*, August–September 1959, pp. 403–14.
Extensive review of Newman's film work. Facts about Newman's work with Chaplin add interest. Includes a filmography.

"Jazz Is Heard at the Movies." *Music U.S.A.*, July 1959, p. 38+.
Extensive review of recent trends in the use of jazz in feature films.

"Johnny Green Tells Duties, Function and Details of Motion Picture Music Director." *Down Beat*, 22 August 1956, p. 13+.
An interview with Green when he was head of the MGM music department, giving a good insight into how the department was run.

Johnson, Julian. "Pandora's Chatterbox." *Saturday Evening Post*, 23 January 1932, pp. 10–11+.
An account of the movie sound department in the 1930s. Interesting historically.

Johnson, William. "Face the Music." *Film Quarterly*, Summer 1969, pp. 3–19.
Excellent article, probably the best survey of film music to appear in a periodical. Traces musical development historically, with valid criticism.

Jordan, William E. "Norman McLaren: His Career and Techniques." *Quarterly of Film, Radio, and Television* 8, no. 1 (Fall 1953): 1–14.
Good description of McLaren's hand-drawn musical sound tracks.

Kallis, Stephen A., Jr. "Background Music by Computer." *American Cinematographer*, November 1971, p. 1148.
A good basic introduction to this new technique and related equipment.

Keller, Hans. "Film Analysis of the Orchestra." *Sight and Sound*, Spring 1947, pp. 30–31.
Critique of short film based on Benjamin Britten's "Young Person's Guide to the Orchestra."

————. "Film Music: Problems of Integration." *Musical Times*, July 1955, pp. 381–82.
An evaluation of film scores.

———. "Film Music: Some Objections." *Sight and Sound,* Winter 1946–47, p. 136.

Adverse criticism of several film scores.

———. "Hollywood Music: Another View." *Sight and Sound,* Spring 1948, pp. 168–69.

Answer to an article by Anthony Thomas in *Sight and Sound.*

Kemp, Jeffrey. "Write What the Film Needs: An Interview with Elisabeth Luytens." *Sight and Sound,* Autumn 1974, pp. 203–48.

Rare interview with distinguished composer of many scores for British documentaries; she enumerates her satisfactions and frustrations.

Kingery, R. A., and R. D. Berg. "The Men Who Taught the Movies How to Speak." *Saturday Review,* April 1968, pp. 56–58. (Reprinted from *Men and Ideas in Engineering.)*

Rather technical, but well-documented, article about sound engineering in motion pictures.

Knight, Arthur. "All Singing! All Talking! All Laughing! 1929, the Year of Great Transition." *Theatre Arts Magazine,* September 1949, pp. 33–40.

Another account of the coming of sound, but a very good one.

———. "Busby Berkeley." *Action* 9, no. 3 (May–June 1974): 11–16.

Career review and analysis of Berkeley's methods.

———. "How the Silents Sounded." *Saturday Review,* 28 May 1960, p. 76.

A review of a record, "Musical Moods for Silent Films," (Golden Crest CR4019), which features famed silent-film accompanist Arthur Kleiner.

Korngold, Julius. "About the Fate of Film Music." *Musical America,* 19 February 1942, pp. 23 + .

Recommendations, rather than predictions; musically valid and sound.

Kreuger, Miles. "The Birth of the American Film Musical." *High Fidelity,* July 1972, pp. 42–48.

A good review of some of the predecessors of the Vitaphone and early musicals of the sound era.

———. "Dubbers to the Stars." *High Fidelity,* July 1972, pp. 49–54.

Who sang for whom in *that* movie musical? Mr. Kreuger names all the names.

Kubik, Gail. "Composing for Government Films." *Modern Music,* Summer 1946, pp. 189–92.
  About the composer's work in wartime OWI films.

Landon, John W. "Long Live the Mighty Wurlitzer." *Journal of Popular Film* 2, no. 1 (Winter 1973): 3–13.
  Traces the evolution of the theater organ, with emphasis on the career of organist Jess Crawford.

Lane, Jerry. "Voice of the Film." *Saturday Evening Post,* 11 March 1933, pp. 10–11 +.
  About the production of movie sound effects.

Lees, Gene. "In Memory of Mercer." *American Film* 2, no. 3, (December–January 1978): 64–65.
  A tribute to the late great lyricist of popular songs and film scores.

————. "New Sounds on the Soundtracks." *High Fidelity* 17 August 1967, p. 58.
  About trends in the 1960s in film music, including the influx of composers from the pop field.

————. "School for Scoring." *American Film* 3, no. 2 (November 1967): 68–69.
  About Pat Williams's program for teaching orchestral techniques, at the University of Colorado.

————. "When the Music Stopped." *High Fidelity/Musical America* 22, no. 7 (July 1972): 20.
  About the composers' strike against the movie producers.

Levinson, Nathan. "What Sound Hath Wrought." *Scientific American,* August 1946, pp. 101–9, and September 1946, pp. 176–90.
  An excellent, fairly technical article. History of sound recording and an explanation of studio sound-engineering techniques. A biographical sketch of Levinson.

Lustig, Milton. "The Music Editor." *Cinemeditor,* Winter 1970–71, pp. 11–12.
  Clear explanation of the music editor's work.

Macgowan, Kenneth. "The Coming of Sound to the Screen." *Quarterly of Film Radio, and Television* 10, no. 2 (Winter 1955): pp. 136–45.
  Early attempts at sound recording in films, pre-Vitaphone, and the work of Sponable and Case, among topics discussed.

————. "When the Talkies Came to Hollywood." *Quarterly of Film, Radio, and Television* 10, no. 3 (Spring 1956): 280–301.
  Excellent account of the early developments of the sound era, and opposition to sound films.

Maffet, James D. *"The Omen—Obsession." Film Music Notebook* 3, no. 1 (1977): 32–44.
About the use of music in films of the supernatural, comparing the music of Bernard Herrmann and Jerry Goldsmith.

Marema, Thomas. "The Sound of Movie Music." *New York Times Magazine,* 28 March 1976, pp. 40–48.
A good review of the work of many "new" composers— Shire, Hamlisch, Baskin, and others, and that of some of the older ones—Herrmann, Rozsa, Korngold, and the contrasts that have emerged.

Margolis, Gary. "Why Soundtrack Albums Don't Sound Better." *High Fidelity,* July 1972, pp. 59–61.
A lucid explanation of what sound engineers do to sound tracks to make them more attractive to record buyers.

Mariani, John. "Music to Cry to Movies By." *Film Comment,* September 1979, p. 37.
A brief review of the return to "sentimental" movie music.

Marsh, Dave. "Schlock around the Rock." *Film Comment* 14, no. 4 (July–August 1978): 7–13.
A survey of rock music movies.

Martin, Pete. "How'll You Have Your Thunder?" *Saturday Evening Post,* 8 September 1945, pp. 14–15.
About the recording of movie sound effects.

Mathieson, Muir. "Developments in Film Music." *Penguin Film Review,* October 1947, pp. 41–46.
Excellent discussion of developments in motion picture music in the previous 15 years.

———. "Music for Crown." *Hollywood Quarterly* 3, no. 3 (Spring 1948): 323–26.
About the work of various composers in documentary films produced by the British government.

McLaren, Norman. "Notes on Animated Sound." *Quarterly of Film, Radio, and Television* 7, no. 3 (Spring 1953): 223–29.
A comprehensible explanation by McLaren of his methods in creating sound tracks.

McNulty, John. "Come Quick, Indians." *Holiday,* January 1953, pp. 22–23.
About piano playing for silent films.

Mermey, Maurice. "The Vanishing Fiddler: The Talkies Threaten Calamity." *North American Review,* December 1929, pp. 301–7.
Prophetic warning about the disappearance of movie theater orchestras.

Milhaud, Darius. "Music for the Film." *Theatre Arts Magazine,* September 1947, pp. 11–14.
Very good analysis of music in a few films.

Moore, Douglas. "Music and the Movies." *Harper's Magazine,* July 1935, pp. 181–88.
An excellent, thoughtful article about the function of motion picture music.

Morton, Lawrence. "Composing, Orchestrating and Criticizing Music for Films." *Quarterly of Film, Radio, and Television* 6, no. 2 (Winter 1951): 191–206.
An extensive and authoritative article on the work of David Raksin, George Duning, and Hugo Friedhofer.

————. "Film Music of the Quarter." *Hollywood Quarterly,* 1945 through 1951; *Quarterly of Film, Radio, and Television,* 1951 through 1953.
A series of articles, all displaying a vast knowledge of motion pictures and musicology, and all worth reading.

Movie
Issue 24, Spring 1977, of the magazine devoted to music in films, including "Entertainment and Utopia," by Richard Dyer, p. 2; "Showmaking," by Denis Giles, p. 14; "Interview with Stanley Donen," by Jim Hollier, p. 26; "The Backstage Musical," by John Belton, p. 36; an article about Disney films (cited under Paul); and "Reviews of Other Films." In all of these articles, however, there is almost no mention of the music in the films that are discussed.

Moving Picture World
A page devoted to the musical accompaniment of silent films appeared in this magazine sporadically, from December 1910 until 1919. Principal authors were Clarence E. Sinn, George W. Beynon, and S. M. Berg. Also of interest: on adjoining pages, advertisements for attachments to musical instruments, designed to provide sound effects and special musical effects in silent film showings.

Murray, William. "The Return of Busby Berkeley." *New York Times Magazine,* 2 March 1969, p. 7 +.
A very good evaluation of Berkeley's films and the entire genre of musicals, as well as an interesting portrait of Berkeley as a person.

Nelson, Gene. "Values of Film Music." *Music Journal,* June 1968, p. 245.
A concise review of musical films by a noted dance director.

Nelson, Robert U. "Film Music: Color or Line?" *Hollywood Quarterly* 2, (October 1946): 57–65.

A musicological analysis of several films. Excellent; interesting from both musical and cinematic standpoints.

"New Film Directors Accenting Music as Potent Dramatic Angle: Alex North." *Variety*, 12 October 1960.
    An interview about trends in film music.

Newlin, Dika. "Music for the Flickering Image." *Music Educators Journal*, September 1977, pp. 24–35.
    Intended mainly for music teachers interested in teaching about film music; discusses the function of music in films.

Newton, Douglas. "Poetry in Fast and Musical Motion." *Sight and Sound*, July 1952, pp. 35–37.
    A slightly different approach to criticism of musical films. Literate and provocative.

Oderman, Stuart. "The Next Tremolo You Hear." *Film Library Quarterly*, Winter 1970–71, p. 54.
    Discusses problems in modern accompaniment of silent films.

"On the Soundtrack." *Down Beat*, beginning 8 August 1957.
    A column, continuing sporadically for about a year.

Orowan, Florella. "A Look at Alex North's Use of Historical Source Music." *Film Music Notebook* 3, no. 1 (1977): 9–14.
    Cites musical examples of *The Agony and the Ecstasy* and *Shoes of the Fisherman*.

Palmer, Christopher. "Focus on Films." *Film Music Notebook*, Summer 1975, pp. 23–30.
    Discussion of the use of familiar music in several recent and older films.

———. "Alex North." *Film Music Notebook*, 3, no. 1 (1977): 2–8.
    A review of North's work; includes a filmography.

———. "Dimitri Tiomkin, a Biographical Sketch." *Film Music Notebook* 4 (1978): 29–34.
    Includes a filmography.

———. "Miklos Rozsa." *Performing Right*, May 1971, pp. 11–15.
    An analysis of some of Rozsa's works.

———. "Miklos Rozsa Biography." *Film Music Notebook* 2, no. 1 (1976): 6–15.
    An excerpt from Palmer's book. Includes a filmography and list of nonfilm works by Rozsa.

———. "Miklos Rozsa on *The Thief of Bagdad*." *Film Music Notebook* 2, no. 4 (1976): 25–28.
    An interview about Rozsa's music for the film.

———. *"The Music of Bernard Herrmann."* Monthly Film Bulletin 43, no. 513 (October 1976): 224.
A tribute to and resume of Herrman's film music, written shortly after Herrmann's death.

———. "The Music of Miklos Rozsa." *Monthly Film Bulletin* 45, no. 530 (March 1978): 60.
Overview, in Palmer's scholarly fashion, of Rozsa's contribution to film music.

———. "Profile of Dimitri Tiomkin." *Performing Right,* May 1970, pp. 24–32.
A review of Tiomkin's film music, and a personality sketch of the composer.

———. "Tiomkin as Russian Composer." *Film Music Notebook* 4 (1978): 35–39.
An offbeat overview of the composer's work.

Parker, David, and Burton J. Shapiro. "The Phonograph Movies." *Association for Recorded Sound Collections—Journal* 7, no. 1–2 (July 1975): 6–20.
"Supplements" Geduld's *The Birth of the Talkies,* and offers corrections.

Paul, William. "Art, Music, Nature, and Walt Disney." *Movie* 24 (Spring 1977): 44–52.
A critique of many Disney films and the function of music in them.

Peck, A. P. "What Makes 'Fantasia' Click: Multiple Sound Tracks and Loudspeakers." *Scientific American,* January 1941, pp. 28–30.
A good, but quite technical article about stereo techniques and problems in projection.

Peebles, Samuel A. "The Mechanical Music Makers." *Films in Review,* April 1973, pp. 193–200.
A different aspect of music for silents: mechanical music instruments and their use in various theaters.

Penn, William. "The Celluloid Image and Mixed Media." *Composer,* no. 4, 1970, p. 179.
A good musical analysis of a few film scores.

Petric, Vlada. "Silence Was Golden." *American Film* 2, no. 10, (September 1977): 64–65.
The problems involved in recent attempts at postsynchronizing musical scores to silents, with details on Chaplin's *A Woman of Paris.*

Pleasants, Henry. "Jazz and the Movies." *World of Music,* no. 3, 1968, pp. 38–47.

Good in-depth consideration of recent trends in music in films, filmed television, and television commercials.

———. "The Screen and the Voice." *Opera News,* 17 January 1970, pp. 8–13.

A review of appearances in films of prominent singers, citing their problems in filming.

Popper, Paul. "Synthetic Sound." *Sight and Sound* 4, no. 14 (1935): 82–84.

A description of "The Sound Manuscript," a method of drawing music and sound effects directly onto the film that may antedate the work of Norman McLaren.

Potamkin, Harry A. "Music and the Movies." *Musical Quarterly,* April 1929, pp. 281–96.

About musical accompaniment of silents.

Potter, Ralph. "Audio-visual Music." *Hollywood Quarterly* 3 (1947): 66–78.

A review of experimental films that employ abstract visual patterns and complementary sound tracks.

Powell, Stephen. "The Mighty Musical Makes Its Comeback." *Millimeter* 7, no. 1 (January 1979): 24–40.

The history of the film musical, and a critique of some recent films, including *Grease* and *The Wiz.*

Pratley, Gerald. "Film Music on Records." *Quarterly of Film, Radio, and Television* 6, no. 1 (Fall 1951), pp. 73–97; vol. 7, no. 1, Fall 1952, pp. 100–107; vol. 8, no. 2, Winter 1953, pp. 194–205; vol. 9, no. 2, Winter 1954, pp. 195–208; vol. 10, no. 2, Winter 1955, pp. 186–207.

Careful, complete listings in each issue.

———. "Furthering Motion Picture Appreciation by Radio." *Hollywood Quarterly* 5, no. 2 (Winter 1950): 127.

Discusses radio programs that featured film music.

Quantrill, Jay Alan. "How Not to Be a Film Critic." *Film Music Notebook* 3, no. 3 (1977): 33–42.

Quantrill takes to task many who write about film music. He states, "They gave film music a bad name."

———. "Jerry Fielding." *Film Music Notebook* 3, no. 3 (1977): 9–17.

A career overview, with a filmography.

Raksin, David. "Whatever Became of Movie Music?" *Film Music Notebook,* 1 Fall 1974, pp. 22–26.

About the state of film music in 1974.

———, with Charles Berg. " 'Music Composed by Charlie Chap-

lin': Auteur or Collaborateur?" *Journal of the University Film Association* 31, no. 1 (Winter 1979): 47–50.
In the form of a letter from Raksin to Berg, Raksin discusses the work of other composers and himself with Charlie Chaplin.

Ramin, Jordan. "Oscar's Songs." *High Fidelity/Musical America*, April 1975, pp. 54–60.
A year-by-year salute to winners and nonwinners of the Academy Awards for songs.

Rapee, Erno. "The Future of Music in Moviedom." *Etude*, September 1929, pp. 649–50+.
Predictions; Rapee saw films as a way to bring good music to the masses.

Robson, Mark. "Why You Hear What You Hear at the Movies." *Good Housekeeping*, July 1955, pp. 99–102.
Good, easily understandable, explanation of sound recording.

Rosar, William. "Lost Horizon." *Film Music Notebook* 4 (1978): 40–52.
An account of the travails of scoring the film, and an analysis of the music.

Rose, Donald. "Silence Is Requested." *North American Review*, July 1930, pp. 127–28.
A petition for the return to silent films, with deprecating criticism of sound pictures.

Rosenman, Leonard. "Notes from a Sub-culture." *Perspectives of New Music*, no. 1, 1968, pp. 122–35.
Serious evaluation of film music, marred by the author's patronizing tone about films in general.

Rubenstein, Lenny. "Composing for Films: An Interview with John Addison." *Cinéaste* 7, no. 2 (Fall 1977): 26–27, 59.
Questions and answers about Addison's career and influences on his work.

Rubsamen, Walter H. "Music in the American Dramatic Film." *Juilliard Review*, Spring 1957, pp. 20–28.
Good review of compositional techniques.

———. "Music in the Cinema." *Arts and Architecture*, April 1944, 9+.
Rather general overview of the use of music in films.

Sarris, Andrew. "The Cultural Guilt of Music Movies." *Film Comment* 13, no. 5 (September–October 1977): 39–41.
A review of the impact of *The Jazz Singer,* and an analysis of Al Jolson as film performer.

Scheff, Michael. "Elmer Bernstein." *Film Music Notebook* 1 (Winter 1974–75): 5–9.
    Career overview and filmography.

Scher, Saul N. "Irving Berlin's Filmusic." *Films in Review,* May 1958, pp. 225–34.
    Review of Berlin's career, with a filmography.

Schiffer, George. "The Law and the Use of Music in Film." *Film Comment,* Fall 1963, pp. 39–43.
    About the licensing of music for film use, from the producer's viewpoint.

Schoenberg, Arnold. "Art and the Moving Picture." *California Arts and Architecture,* April 1940, p. 12 +.
    About films rather than about music, but worth reading.

Schreger, Charles. "The Second Coming of Sound." *Film Comment* 14, no. 5 (September–October 1978): 34–37.
    Compares the advent of sound films in 1927–28 with the "great obsession" with sound in America today, not only in films but in FM radio, Musak, etc.

Seldes, Gilbert. "Theory about Talkies." *New Republic,* 28 August 1928, pp. 305–6.
    Seldes admits to prejudices against talkies, then rips them apart.

Sharples, Win. "The Aesthetics of Film Sound." *Filmmakers Newsletter* 8, no. 5 (March 1975): 27–32.
    Thoughtful, provocative study of the relationship of sound (including music) and the film image. Discusses background and source music, and the functions of each.

———. "Cinescenes: Bernard Herrmann, 1911–75." *Filmmakers Newsletter* 9, no. 12 (October 1976): 12.
    A tribute to the late composer.

———. "Explorations: Love's Labour Found." *American Film* 1, no. 5 (March 1976): 68–71.
    About the work of the Elmer Bernstein Film Collection and the Miklos Rozsa Society.

Shavin, Norman. "Them Days Is Gone Forever." *Music Journal,* March 1954, p. 13 +.
    About musical accompaniment of silents.

Shepard, David. "Silent Music." *American Film Institute Report,* 1972, no. 1, p. 3.
    An introductory review of silent-film accompaniments, with recommendations of books on the subject.

Siders, Henry. "Meet Pat Williams." *Down Beat,* 4 March 1971, p. 20 +.

An interview, mostly about Williams's film work.

"Sir William Walton's Shakespeare Film Scores." *American Record Guide,* May 1964, pp. 881–83.
Résumé of Walton's film work and list of recordings.

"Sound-proof Studios for Talkies." *Literary Digest,* 12 January 1929, p. 19.
About problems of early sound film recording. Interesting as history.

"The Sound Track." *Films in Review,* beginning March 1968.
A monthly column, published quite regularly up to the present time. Page Cook is the most frequent contributor.

Spolar, Betsey, and Merrilyn Hammond. "How to Work in Hollywood and Still Be Happy." *Theatre Arts Magazine,* August 1953, p. 80.
About Alex North, his film work and personal views.

Stamelman, Peter. "Film Composer David Shire." *Millimeter* 4, no. 4 (April 1976): 20–21.
A profile, in which Shire discusses his film scores and other aspects of his career.

Steiner, Fred. "Bernard Herrmann." *Film Music Notebook,* Summer 1975, pp. 4–9. (Reprinted, vol. 3, no. 2 (1977), pp. 6–11, with a "postscript.")
An overview of Herrmann's career, with a filmography and list of orchestral compositions.

―――. "An Examination of Leith Stevens' Use of Jazz in *The Wild One.*" *Film Music Notebook,* part 1, vol. 2, no. 2 (1976), pp. 26–35; part 2, vol. 2, no. 3 (1976), pp. 26–34.
Analysis of background and source music in the film, and a review of the use of jazz in previous films.

―――. "Herrmann's 'Black and White' Music for Hitchcock's *Psycho.*" *Film Music Notebook,* part 1, vol. 1 (Fall 1974), pp. 26–46; part 2, vol. 1 (Winter 1974–75), pp. 28–36.
In-depth musicological analysis.

Stern, Seymour. "The Film's Score." *Film Culture,* no. 36, Spring 1965, pp. 103–32.
Interesting as part of an issue devoted to *The Birth of a Nation,* in its description of the film's score and critical and audience reaction to it. Style is flamboyant, almost hysterical, in an emotional critique of Joseph Carl Breil and his music.

Sternfield, Frederick W. "Copland as Film Composer." *Musical Quarterly,* April 1950, pp. 517–32.
A musicologist's evaluation, very well written.

———. "Music and the Feature Film." *Musical Quarterly,* October 1947, pp. 517–32.

An excellent musicological analysis of the work of Hugo Friedhofer, particularly his score for *The Best Years of Our Lives.*

Stockton, Ann Mason, and Dorothy Remsen. "Motion Picture Recording." *American Harp Journal,* no. 2, 1967, pp. 8–9.

A discussion of some of the problems of recording this instrument for films, from the performer's viewpoint.

Stokowski, Leopold. "My Symphonic Debut in the Films." *Etude,* November 1936, pp. 685–86.

An enthusiastic description of the conductor's appearance in *The Big Broadcast of 1937.*

Stothart, Herbert, Jr. "Herbert Stothart Was a Pioneer of Film Makers." *Films in Review,* December 1970, 622–42.

A nostalgic look at MGM's golden musical days.

Sutak, Ken. "The Investment Market: Movie Music Albums." *High Fidelity,* July 1972, pp. 62–66.

A guide to the realized prices of rare sound-track albums.

Thomas, Anthony. "David Raksin." *Films in Review,* January 1963, pp. 38–41.

A career biography, with filmography. Some material about Raksin's work with Chaplin and studies with Schoenberg.

———. "Erich Wolfgang Korngold." *Films in Review,* February 1965, pp. 89–90.

Review of career.

———. "Hollywood Music." *Sight and Sound,* Autumn 1947, pp. 97–98.

About the work of several composers, including Miklos Rozsa and Max Steiner.

———. "Hugo Friedhofer." *Films in Review,* October 1965, pp. 496–510.

Extensive, thorough biography/career article, with filmography.

Tiomkin, Dimitri. "Composing for Films." *Films in Review,* November 1951, pp. 17–22.

The composer's review of his career.

———. "The Music of Hollywood." *Music Journal,* November–December 1962, p. 7 + .

A statement about the value of film music.

———. "Writing Symphonically for the Screen." *Music Journal,* January 1959, p. 26 + .

Discusses some of the composer's many films.

Tossi, R. V. "Jerome Kern's Film Music." *Films in Review,* November 1955, 452–59.
A biography and career overview, with a filmography.

Traubner, Richard. "The Sound and the Führer." *Film Comment,* July–August, 1978, pp. 17–23.
Evaluation of musical films made in Nazi Germany.

Tynan, John. "Take Five—Jazz in Motion Pictures." *Down Beat,* 8 January 1959, pp. 42–43.
Brief review of the subject.

Uselton, Roi A. "Opera Singers on the Screen." *Films in Review,* part 1, April 1967, pp. 193–206; part 2, May 1967, pp. 284–97.
A very complete review of opera stars' film roles, even in the silents.

Vallance, Tom. "Melody Always Wins." *Focus on Film* 21 (Summer 1975): 14–26.
A career interview with songwriter Jule Styne, with candid answers to questions about his film work.

Varèse, Edgard. "Organized Sound Film." *Commonweal,* 13 December 1940, pp. 204–5.
One of music's most famous iconoclasts presents his ideas about films, present and future. A most interesting article.

Vaughan Williams, Ralph. "Film Music." *Film Music Notebook* 2, no. 2 (1976): 22–35.
Reprint of an article which appeared in *Film Music Notes,* 1944. A statement of Vaughan Williams's philosophy concerning film music.

"Warner Brothers Rode to Success on Wave of Sound." *Newsweek,* 26 December 1936, pp. 23–26.
An account of the Warners' successful gamble on sound, and subsequent economic health.

Warshow, Paul. "More Is Less: Comedy and Sound." *Film Quarterly,* 31, no. 1 (Fall 1977): 38–45.
The use and misuse of sound effects and music in modern-day postsynchronized silent comedies, specifically the Buster Keaton classics.

Weill, Kurt. "Music in the Movies." *Harper's Bazaar,* September 1946, pp. 257, 398–400.
Discussion in terms of the composer's problems in writing for films. Good ideas and literate writing.

Whitaker, Rod. "The Role of Movie Music." *Music Journal Annual,* 1966, p. 68 +.
A historical review of the subject.

Winkler, Max. "The Origins of Film Music." *Films in Review,* December 1951, pp. 34–42.
An excerpt from his book.

Winter, Marion H. "Function of Music in the Sound Film." *Musical Quarterly,* April 1941, pp. 146–64.
A good discussion of musical aesthetics, and analysis of early landmark sound films.

Wood, Robin. "Never Never Change, Always Gonna Dance." *Film Comment,* September–October 1979, pp. 28–31.
A scholarly, but not pedantic, analysis of the charms of Fred Astaire and Ginger Rogers and their movies.

"The World and the Theater: Research in Sound Reproduction." *Theatre Arts Monthly,* March 1930, pp. 185–89.
Quotes from Pudovkin about his work in early sound films, and his theories.

Wright, Basil. "Britten and Documentary." *Musical Times,* November 1963, pp. 779–80.
Good review of the composer's work.

Yates, Raymond F. "A Technician Talks about the Talkies." *Scientific American,* November 1930, pp. 384–85.
Problems of sound recording reviewed in practical terms.

Stars of Musical Films: Biographies and Books About Their Films

Julie Andrews

Cotrell, John. *Julie Andrews: The Unauthorized Life Story of a Super-Star.* New York: Dell, 1968. 212 pp.

Windeler, Robert. *Julie Andrews: A Biography.* New York: G. P. Putnam's Sons, 1970. 253 pp.

Fred Astaire

Astaire, Fred. *Steps in Time.* New York: Harper and Brothers, 1959. 338 pp.

Croce, Arlene, *The Fred Astaire and Ginger Rogers Book.* Nw York: Outerbridge and Hazard, 1972. 191 pp.

Freedland, Michael. *Fred Astaire.* London: W. H. Allen, 1976. 277 pp.

Green, Benny. *Fred Astaire.* New York: Exeter Books, 1979, 176 pp.

Green, Stanley, and Burt Goldblatt. *Starring Fred Astaire.* New York: Dodd, Mead, 1973. 501 pp.

Hackl, Alfons. *Fred Astaire and His Work.* Vienna: Edition Austria International, 1970. 120 pp.

Harvey, Stephen. *Fred Astaire.* New York: Pyramid, 1975. 158 pp.

Smith, Milburn, ed. *Astaire and Rogers.* New York: A. S. Barnes and Co., 1972. 66 pp.

Thompson, Howard. *Fred Astaire: A Pictorial Treasury of His Films.* New York: Falcon, 1970. 154 pp.

Topper, Susanne. *Astaire and Rogers.* New York: Leisure Books, 1976. 206 pp.

Eddie Cantor

Cantor, Eddie. *As I Remember Them.* New York: Duell, Sloan and Pearce, 1963. 144 pp.

————, as told to David Freedman. *My Life Is in Your Hands.* New York: Blue Ribbon Books, 1932. 309 pp.

————. *The Way I See It.* Englewood Cliffs, N.J.: Prentice-Hall, 1959. 204 pp.

————, with Jane Kesner Ardmore. *Take My Life.* Garden City, N.Y.: Doubleday, 1957. 288 pp.

Maurice Chevalier

Chevalier, Maurice. *I Remember It Well.* New York: Macmillan Co., 1970. 221 pp.

————. *The Man in the Straw Hat: My Story.* New York: Thomas Y. Crowell Co., 1949. 245 pp.

————, as told to Eileen and Robert Mason Pollack. *With Love.* Boston: Little, Brown and Co., 1960. 424 pp.

Cudlipp, Percy. *Maurice Chevalier's Own Story.* London: Nash and Grayson, 1930. 93 pp.

Ringgold, Gene, and DeWitt Bodeen. *Chevalier: The Films and Career of Maurice Chevalier.* Secaucus, N.J.: Citadel Press, 1973. 245 pp.

Bing Crosby

Bauer, Barbara. *Bing Crosby.* New York: Pyramid, 1977. 159 pp.

Bookbinder, Robert. *The Films of Bing Crosby.* Secaucus, N.J.: Citadel Press, 1977. 256 pp.

Carpozi, George, Jr. *The Fabulous Life of Bing Crosby.* New York: Pyramid, 1977. 159 pp.

Crosby, Bing, with Pete Martin. *Call Me Lucky.* New York: Simon and Schuster, 1953. 334 pp.

Crosby, Kathryn. *Bing and Other Things.* New York: Meredith, 1967. 214 pp.

Crosby, Ted. *The Story of Bing Crosby.* Cleveland: World, 1946. 239 pp. (Originally published 1937, with authors listed as Ted Crosby and Larry Crosby.)

Thomas, Bob. *The One and Only Bing.* New York: Grosset and Dunlap, 1977. 151 pp.

Thompson, Charles. *Bing: The Authorized Biography.* London: W. H. Allen, 1975. 249 pp.

Ulanov, Barry. *The Incredible Crosby.* New York: Whittlesey, 1948. 336 pp.

Zwison, Laurance, J. *Bing Crosby: A Lifetime of Music.* Los Angeles, Calif.: Palm Tree Library, 1978. 147 pp.

Sammy Davis, Jr.

Davis, Sammy, Jr. *Hollywood in a Suitcase.* New York: William Morrow and Company, 1980. 288 pp.

Davis, Sammy, Jr., with Jane and Burt Boyar. *Yes, I Can: The Story of Sammy Davis, Jr.* New York: Farrar, Straus and Giroux, 1965. 612 pp.

Doris Day

Day, Doris, with A. E. Hotchner. *Doris Day: Her Own Story.* New York: William Morrow and Company, 1975. 313 pp.

Gelb, Alan. *The Doris Day Scrapbook.* New York: Grosset and Dunlap, 1977. 158 pp.

Morris, George. *Doris Day.* New York: Pyramid, 1976. 159 pp.

Thomas, Ted. *Doris Day: The Dramatic Story of America's Number One Box Office Star.* Derby, Conn.: Monarch Books, 1962. 139 pp.

Young, Christopher. *The Films of Doris Day.* Secaucus, N.J.: Citadel Press, 1977. 253 pp.

Nelson Eddy

Castanza, Phillip. *The Films of Jeanette MacDonald and Nelson Eddy.* Secaucus, N.J.: Citadel, 1975. 469 pp.

Goodrich, Diane. *Farewell to Dreams.* Hollywood, Calif.: Jeanette MacDonald/Nelson Eddy Friendship Club, 1979. 291 pp.

Knowles, Eleanor. *The Films of Jeanette MacDonald and Nelson Eddy.* South Brunswick, N.J.: A. S. Barnes and Co., 1975. 469 pp.

Alice Faye

Moshier, W. Franklyn. *The Films of Alice Faye.* San Francisco; W. Franklyn Moshier, 1971. 194 pp. (Reprinted as *The Alice Faye Movie Book.* Harrisburg, Pa.: Stackpole, 1974.)

Judy Garland

Dahl, David, and Barry Kehoe. *Young Judy.* New York: Mason/Charter, 1975. 250 pp.

Deans, Mickey, and Ann Pinchot. *Weep No More, My Lady.* New York: Hawthorn, 1972. 247 pp.

Di Orio, Al. *Little Girl Lost: The Life and Hard Times of Judy Garland.* New York: Barven, 1972. 298 pp.

Edwards, Anne. *Judy Garland: A Biography.* New York: Simon and Schuster, 1975. 349 pp.

Finch, Christopher. *Rainbow: The Stormy Life of Judy Garland.* New York: Grosset and Dunlap, 1975. 255 pp.

Frank, Gerold. *Judy.* New York: Harper and Row, 1975. 654 pp.

Juneau, James. *Judy Garland.* New York: Pyramid, 1974. 159 pp.

Melton, David. *Judy: A Remembrance.* Hollywood, Calif.: Stanyan, 1972. 58 pp.

Morella, Joe, and Edward Epstein. *Judy: The Films and Career of Judy Garland.* New York: Citadel Press, 1969. 217 pp.

Smith, Lorna. *Judy with Love: The Story of Miss Show Business.* London: Hale, 1975. 208 pp.

Smith, Milburn, ed. *Judy Garland and Mickey Rooney.* New York: Barven, 1972. 66 pp.

Steiger, Brad. *Judy Garland.* New York: Ace Publishing Co., 1969. 150 pp.

Torme, Mel. *The Other Side of the Rainbow with Judy Garland of the Dawn Patrol.* New York: William Morrow and Company, 1970. 241 pp.

Sonja Henie

Henie, Sonja. *Wings on My Feet.* New York: Prentice-Hall, 1940. 177 pp.

Bob Hope

Hope, Bob, as told to Pete Martin. *Have Tux, Will Travel.* New York: Simon and Schuster, 1954. 308 pp.

Morella, Joe and Edward Z. Epstein and Eleanor Clark. *The Amazing Careers of Bob Hope.* New Rochelle, N.Y.: Arlington House, 1973. 256 pp.

Lena Horne

Horne, Lena, with Helen Arnstein and Carlton Moss. *In Person, Lena Horne.* New York: Greenberg, 1950. 249 pp.

————, and Richard Schickel. *Lena.* Garden City, N.Y.: Doubleday, 1965. 300 pp.

Al Jolson

Abramson, Martin. *The Real Story of Al Jolson.* New York: Spectrolux, 1950. 48 pp.

Freedland, Michael. *Jolson.* New York: Stein and Day, 1972. 256 pp. (Also published as *Al Jolson.*)

Jolson, Harry, with Alban Emley. *Mistah Jolson.* Hollywood, Calif.: House-Warren, 1951. 257 pp.

Sieben, Pearl. *The Immortal Jolson: His Life and Times.* New York: Fell, 1942. 231 pp.

Danny Kaye

Richards, Dick. *The Life Story of Danny Kaye.* London: Convoy, 1949. 70 pp.

Singer, Kurt. *The Danny Kaye Story.* New York: Nelson, 1958. 241

pp. (Published in London as *The Danny Kaye Saga*. Robert Hale, 1957. 206 pp.)

Gene Kelly

Basinger, Jeanine. *Gene Kelly*. New York: Pyramid, 1976. 160 pp.

Burrows, Michael. *Gene Kelly: Versatility Personified*. Cornwall, England: Primestyle, 1972. 40 pp.

Griffith, Richard. *The Cinema of Gene Kelly*. New York: The Museum of Modern Art Film Library, 1962. 16 pp.

Hirschhorn, Clive. *Gene Kelly: A Biography*. Chicago: Henry Regnery, 1975. 335 pp.

Thomas, Tony. *The Films of Gene Kelly, Song and Dance Man*. Secaucus, N.J.: Citadel, 1974.

Dorothy Lamour

Lamour, Dorothy, as told to Dick McInnes. *My Side of the Road*. Englewood Cliffs, N.J.: Prentice-Hall, 1980. 244 pp.

Jeanette MacDonald

Castanza, Phillip. *The Films of Jeanette MacDonald and Nelson Eddy*. Secaucus, N.J.: Citadel Press, 1975. 469 pp.

Goodrich, Diane. *Farewell to Dreams*. Hollywood, Calif.: Jeanette MacDonald/Nelson Eddy Friendship Club, 1979. 291 pp.

Knowles, Eleanor. *The Films of Jeanette MacDonald and Nelson Eddy*. South Brunswick, N.J.: A. S. Barnes and Co., 1975. 469 pp.

Parish, James Robert. *The Jeanette MacDonald Story*. New York: Mason /Charter, 1976. 181 pp.

Rich, Sharon. *Jeanette MacDonald: A Pictorial Treasury*. Los Angeles, Calif.: Times-Mirror Press, 1973. 253 pp.

Stern, Lee Edward. *Jeanette MacDonald*. New York: Harbrace, 1977.

Jessie Matthews

Matthews, Jessie, with Muriel Burgess. *Over My Shoulder: An Autobiography*. New Rochelle, N.Y.: Arlington House, 1975. 240 pp.

Thornton, Michael. *Jessie Matthews: A Biography.* London: Hart-Davis, MacGibbon, 1974. 359 pp.

Ann Miller

Miller, Ann, with Norma Lee Browning. *Miller's High Life.* Garden City, N.Y.: Doubleday, 1972. 283 pp.

Liza Minnelli

D'Arcy, Susan. *The Films of Liza Minnelli.* London: Barnden Castell Williams, 1973. 47 pp.

Parish, James Robert, with Jack Ano. *Liza! An Unauthorized Biography.* New York: Pocket Books, 1975. 176 pp.

Grace Moore

Moore, Grace. *You're Only Human Once.* Garden City, N.Y.: Doubleday, Doran and Co., 1944. 275 pp.

George Murphy

Murphy, George, with Victor Lasky. *"Say . . . Didn't You Used to Be George Murphy?"* New York: Bartholomew House, 1970. 438 pp.

Elvis Presley

Bowser, James, ed. *Starring Elvis.* New York: Dell, 1977. 255 pp.

Dunleavy, Steve, et al. *Elvis: What Happened?* New York: Ballantine Books, 1977. 332 pp.

Grove, Martin. *Elvis: The Legend Lives.* New York: Manor Books, 1978. 256 pp.

———. *The King is Dead: Elvis Presley.* New York: Manor Books, 1977. 252 pp.

Hopkins, Jerry. *Elvis.* New York: Simon and Schuster, 1971. 448 pp.

James, Anthony. *Presley: Entertainer of the Century.* New York: Belmont Tower, 1976. 224 pp.

Lacker, Marty, et al. *Elvis, Portrait of a Friend.* Memphis, Tenn.: Wimmer Brothers, 1979. 369 pp.

Lichter, Paul. *Elvis in Hollywood.* New York: Simon and Schuster, 1975. 188 pp.

Mann, May. *Elvis and the Colonel.* New York: Drake Publishers, 1975. 273 pp.

Zmijewsky, Steven, and Boris Zmijewsky. *Elvis: The Films and Career of Elvis Presley.* Secaucus, N.J.: Citadel Press, 1976. 224 pp.

Paul Robeson

Freedomways, the editors of. *Paul Robeson, the Great Forerunner.* New York: Dodd, Mead, and Co., 1978. 383 pp.

Gilliam, Virginia. *Paul Robeson: All-American.* Washington, D.C.: The New Republic Book Co., 1976. 216 pp.

Graham, Shirley. *Paul Robeson: Citizen of the World.* New York: J. Messner, 1946. 264 pp.

Hamilton, Virginia. *Paul Robeson: The Life and Times of a Free Black Man.* New York: Harper and Row, 1974. 217 pp.

Hoyt, Edwin P. *Paul Robeson: The American Othello.* New York: World, 1967. 288 pp.

Robeson, Eslanda Goode. *Paul Robeson, Negro.* London: Victor Gollancz, 1930. 153 pp.

Seton, Marie. *Paul Robeson.* London: Dennis Dobson, 1958. 254 pp.

Ginger Rogers

Croce, Arlene. *The Fred Astaire and Ginger Rogers Book.* New York: Outerbridge and Hazard, 1972. 191 pp.

Dickens, Homer. *The Films of Ginger Rogers.* Secaucus, N.J.: Citadel Press, 1975. 256 pp.

McGilligan, Patrick. *Ginger Rogers.* New York: Pyramid, 1975. 159 pp.

Richards, Dick. *Ginger: Salute to a Star.* Brighton, England: Clifton, 1968. 192 pp.

Smith, Milburn. *Astaire and Rogers.* New York: A. S. Barnes and Co., 1972. 66 pp.

Topper, Susanne. *Astaire and Rogers.* New York: Leisure Books, 1976. 206 pp.

Mickey Rooney

Rooney, Mickey. *I. E.: The Autobiography of Mickey Rooney.* New York: G. P. Putnam's Sons, 1965. 249 pp.

Smith, Milburn, ed. *Judy Garland and Mickey Rooney.* New York: Barven, 1972. 66 pp.

Diana Ross

Berman, Connie. *Diana Ross—Supreme Lady.* New York: Popular Library, 1978. 174 pp.

Frank Sinatra

Barnes, Ken, with Stan Britt and others. *Sinatra and the Great Song Stylists.* London: Allan, 1972. 192 pp.

Douglas-Home, Robin. *Sinatra.* New York: Grosset and Dunlap, 1962. 64 pp.

Dwiggins, Don. *Hollywood's Loveable Rogue: Frankie, the Life and Loves of Frank Sinatra.* New York: Paperback Library, 1961. 156 pp.

Frank, Alan. *Sinatra.* New York: Leon Amiel Publisher, 1978. 176 pp.

Gehman, Richard. *Sinatra and His Rat Pack.* New York: Belmont, 1961. 220 pp.

Kahn, E. J., Jr. *The Voice: The Story of an American Phenomenon.* New York: Harper and Brothers, 1947. 125 pp.

Lonstein, Albert I, and Vito R. Marino. *The Compleat Sinatra: Discography, Filmography, Television, Motion Picture, Radio, Concert and Stage Appearances.* Ellenville, N.Y.: Cameron Publications, 1970. 383 pp.

Ringgold, Gene, and Clifford McCarty. *The Films of Frank Sinatra.* New York: Citadel Press, 1971. 249 pp.

Sciacci, Tony. *Sinatra.* New York: Pinnacle Books, 1976. 248 pp.

Shaw, Arnold. *Sinatra: Twentieth-Century Romantic.* New York: Holt, Rinehart and Winston, 1968. 371 pp.

Wilson, Earl. *Sinatra, an Authorized Biography.* New York: Macmillan Co., 1976. 357 pp.

Barbra Streisand

Black, Jonathan. *Streisand.* New York: Leisure Books, 1975. 187 pp.

Castell, David. *The Films of Barbra Streisand.* London: Barnden Castell Williams, 1974. 47 pp.

Jordan, Réne. *The Greatest Star: The Barbra Streisand Story,* An *Unauthorized Biography.* New York: G. P. Putnam's Sons, 1975. 253 pp.

Spada, James. *Barbra, The First Decade: The Films and Career of Barbra Streisand.* Secaucus, N.J.: Citadel Press, 1974. 224 pp.

Shirley Temple

Basinger, Jeanine. *Shirley Temple.* New York: Pyramid, 1975. 160 pp.

Beatty, Jerome. *Shirley Temple. Authorized Edition.* Akron, Ohio: Saalfield Publishing Company, 1935. 107 pp.

Burdick, Loraine. *The Shirley Temple Scrapbook.* Middle Village, N.Y.: Jonathan David, 1975. 160 pp.

Eby, Lois. *Shirley Temple: The Amazing Story.* Derby, Conn.: Monarch, 1962. 143 pp.

Temple, Shirley, and the editors of *Look. My Young Life.* Garden City, N.Y.: Garden City Publishing Company, 1945. 253 pp.

Windeler, Robert. *The Films of Shirley Temple.* Secaucus, N.J.: Citadel Press, 1978.

Index

Note: Photographs are indicated by italicized numbers.

186